Reading CPE

Eight practice tests for the **Cambridge C2 Proficiency**

Fiona Aish
and Jo Tomlinson

PROSPERITY EDUCATION

Registered offices: Sherlock Close, Cambridge
CB3 OHP, United Kingdom

First published 2021

ISBN: 978-1-91-382538-6

Cover design and typesetting by ORP Cambridge

For further information and resources, visit:
www.prosperityeducation.net

To infinity and beyond.

Contents

Introduction

Welcome to this edition of sample tests for the Cambridge C2 Proficiency (CPE), Reading (Parts 5–7).

This resource comprises eight whole Reading tests, detailed answer keys and write-in answer sheets.

The content has been written to closely replicate the Cambridge exam experience, and has undergone comprehensive expert and peer review. You or your students, if you are a teacher, will hopefully enjoy the wide range of text topics and benefit from the repetitive practice, something that is key to preparing for this part of the C2 Proficiency (CPE) examination.

We hope that you will find this resource a useful study aid, and we wish you all the best in preparing for the exam.

Fiona Aish and Jo Tomlinson
Spain, 2021

Fiona Aish and Jo Tomlinson are directors of Target English, a consultancy in Spain that provides tailor-made solutions in content creation, course provision, training and testing.

Other titles for the C2 Proficiency

Visit www.prosperityeducation.net to view our wide selection of Cambridge exam resources (B2–C2).

Reading CPE
Eight practice tests for the Cambridge C2 Proficiency

Fiona Aish and Jo Tomlinson

CPE Parts 5–7

2021

978-1913825386

100 pages

Use of English
Ten more practice tests for the Cambridge C2 Proficiency

Fiona Aish and Jo Tomlinson

CPE Parts 1–4

2021

978-1913825478

100 pages

Use of English
Ten practice tests for the Cambridge C2 Proficiency

Michael Macdonald

CPE Parts 1–4

2020

978-1916129733

100 pages

Cambridge C2 Proficiency Reading: Parts 5–7

Test 1

You are going to read an extract from an article. For questions 31–36, mark the appropriate answer (A, B, C or D) that you think fits best according to the text.

The Lost Art of Diplomacy

What it can do for you and why society needs to harness its values

The twentieth century has frequently been labelled as the age of opinion, and not necessarily in a positive way, as any quick glance at social media will demonstrate. In fact, look more closely into the insults traded on social media platforms and the sensationalist ways in which the media presents differing public opinions as polarising, and the situation starts to look even worse. The modern world can often feel rude, and people often behave as though they are totally unwilling to consider, or even listen to, views that are not aligned with their own. It appears that a change is long overdue, and perhaps diplomacy could be the answer to turning this situation around.

Developed over millennia as a way to mediate between grumpy leaders hell-bent on inflicting their own ideas on the world, diplomacy was once thought of as an art, in the same vein as public speaking, polite conversation and negotiation. It grew out of trade interactions in the Middle East, China and India, and incorporated a variety of skills, philosophies and cultural nuances as it went. Throughout the majority of history, the role of the diplomat was to convey information and messages and negotiate in less inflammatory ways than their leaders might have done. These leaders could quite easily justify starting wars in the heat of the moment due to a perceived personal attack from an enemy. In short, they sought to ensure any interaction with another state or power remained on an even keel and avoided conflict at all costs.

Although the word 'diplomacy' conjures up a long-gone age of stuffy meetings between politicians and civil servants in palaces and embassies, there is little difference in the goal of diplomacy nowadays. For example, in the complex relationships of modern society, whether in our personal lives, in the workplace or matters of international negotiation, bringing back the art of diplomacy could be invaluable. It is a highly specific skill that requires people to put aside their personal desires and work towards a common good. In this respect it is extremely challenging insofar as it involves putting forward a case for something strongly and effectively enough for it to be considered by another party, but not in such a way as to cause offence or irritation. As the British journalist and writer David Frost once said, "Diplomacy is the art of letting somebody else have your way."

We are inclined to view diplomacy as an innate ability, something that only a select few are blessed with. Yet, with some hard work and determination it is actually straightforward to learn. For people who make a special effort, the benefits will very soon become apparent. There are, as one would expect, certain tricks of the trade that can be useful starting places for novices. The greatest of these is the ability to understand the fragility of human nature and the need for acceptance and for an attentive audience. This is often the underlying cause of arguments as well as being a plausible explanation for much of the verbal abuse found online today. Being diplomatic means acknowledging the feelings of others, taking time to demonstrate empathy, and casting aside emotion for logic and reasonableness. It means being patient and versatile in interpersonal communication, and, above all, a commitment to agreement and collaboration rather than individuality and division.

Having said this, there are people who seem to naturally excel at diplomatic negotiation and perhaps they are the ones who can shed light on its benefits. These individuals are people who have already understood the human condition in all its frailty. Diplomats are in essence realists who know full well that relationships, families, jobs and nations will face countless problems. They have accepted this with an air of optimistic resignation and believe that compromise is the only antidote to an imperfect world. As such they represent an alternative route to happiness and shared understanding. Despite the outward appearance of pessimism and negativity, they aspire to create a better world and see great progress in small adjustments. They are the undeniable evidence that diplomacy has a lot to offer in illuminating a path to better communication for all of us.

31 What is the writer's purpose in the first paragraph?

A To suggest that the media is manipulating people.

B To provide examples of intolerance in modern society.

C To outline the problems caused by social media.

D To encourage better manners in public places.

32 In paragraph 2, what is the writer's opinion of diplomats?

A Their influence used to be excessive.

B They have become less important.

C Their role is not easy to justify.

D They have always been extremely valuable.

33 In paragraph 3, what does the writer imply about diplomacy?

A It's beneficial for interpersonal communication.

B It's an out-of-date mode of interaction.

C It's not a worthwhile skill for modern society.

D It's an effective technique for political negotiation.

34 In paragraph 4, the writer says that developing our diplomatic skills is:

A easier for more emotional people.

B something everyone should aspire to.

C too time-consuming for modern life.

D well worth investing the time and effort.

35 In paragraph 5, according to the writer, how do successful diplomats view the world?

A They are optimistic about the human condition.

B They believe that people should try to overcome suffering.

C They approach life from a practical perspective.

D They think that the search for happiness is pointless.

36 What is the main point that the writer wants to make in the article?

A A reintroduction of the art of diplomacy would create a more equal society based on tolerance.

B Diplomacy is probably the best approach to resolving the fractured nature of society.

C Interpersonal skills related to diplomacy could have a positive impact on society.

D While diplomacy has positives, people should be wary of its appropriateness in all contexts.

You are going to read an extract from an article. Seven paragraphs have been removed. Select from the paragraphs (A–H) the one that fits each gap (37–43). There is one extra paragraph that you do not need to use.

More to History than Books

Most young people are far more interested in their social circles and the latest fashion and technology crazes than they are about hearing about the past, but for me, local heritage has always been something I've found fascinating. It also, in my mind, holds great importance simply because if we don't make efforts to unearth experiences of the past from others, they will end up being lost in the mists of time.

37	

"I remember it as if it were yesterday. There we all were, standing outside in our slippers and dressing gowns, watching the flames dance in the night sky over the rooftops. The whole area was lit up like a Christmas tree, and we could feel the heat from over a mile away. That night I watched the great building whose shadow I'd lived under all my life disappear before my very eyes. By morning, there was nothing."

38	

Originally situated in Hyde Park, it was erected temporarily as a celebration of the Industrial Revolution, but, due to its overwhelming success, the exhibition was later relocated to a park in south London, where it remained until the great fire of 1936 razed it to the ground in just a few hours. Today, there are few signs that this incredible building ever existed.

39	

Londoners in the 1800s had little time for such preoccupations, but the Crystal Palace gave people a wonderful opportunity to explore ideas of the past and future, as well as to experience the wonders of modern industry. Standing over 40 metres tall and around half a kilometre wide, the glass megastructure housed many different types of museum exhibits from around the globe as well as a music hall, a park and a theatre.

40	

"That's not to say it wasn't an impressive sight. I think the upkeep was just too much to be honest. It's a shame really. I seem to remember there were plans to auction it off to whoever would pay the most, which kicked up quite a fuss at the time with local residents, as you can imagine."

41	

For me, this is perhaps one of the saddest elements of all. Although added to keep the history of the palace alive, it attracts very few people and is located in a somewhat obscure area of the park. Apart from the odd school visit and a few local-history fanatics, this great treasure is frequently overlooked by locals and visitors alike.

42	

In my mind, social first-hand histories are so important for this very reason. While even my grandmother can't recall the glory days of the Crystal Palace, her mother would have been alive to witness them, and if these recollections had been passed on and properly documented, we would be able to paint a more vivid picture of a place that was fundamental in the development of the local area.

43	

After all, we can learn facts and figures from public records and textbooks, but these cannot convey what it was actually like to live though such events. Only with the people who experienced them, who for the first time could travel around the world without ever leaving home and could wonder at marvels of modern industry beyond their wildest dreams.

A The only remnants of this one-time marvel are the dinosaur replicas that still exist around the lakes within the park. Of course, these days they look a little quaint and aren't exactly true to life, but we have to remember that they were built around 150 years ago when relatively little was known of natural history.

B The cost of maintenance and depressed admission prices meant that in the 1900s maintenance was unattended to and the palace was in financial dire straits. It was restored by the Earl of Plymouth who bought the structure in the 1920s in order to preserve it. This brought back visitors and renewed profit, through events such as 'Thursday evening fireworks' and motor shows.

C Perhaps this is due to a lack of general awareness of the true scale and greatness of the palace. After all, it was thriving at a time when film was in its infancy, so we cannot even imagine what it might have been like inside, and still photos don't give us the sense of atmosphere that we can get from video and narratives.

D My grandmother's recollections were a far cry from this though: "All of that was long gone by the time I was little. We'd still go up there as a family, but the building and grounds were getting a bit run down. I think its prime was in the late 1800s, before I was born."

E Mindful of this, the long chats I had with my grandparents will always remain dear to my heart, specifically my grandmother's recollections of her youth. Despite being in her nineties by the time I was of an age to fully understand and ask about her life, she was still sharp as a pin and could answer in such a way that brought the past to life.

F Our parents and grandparents should be encouraged to tell their histories and to write them down. Historians are not just academics; they are everyday people like you and me. History books may tell us about dates, names and major events, but we maintain the richness of feeling that comes from personal accounts.

G Fortunately, the Earl of Plymouth acquired the palace and grounds in order to protect it and the site is now a public park, still used by many throughout the year for numerous sports events as well as much smaller-scale music and cultural festivals. Within the grounds there is even a small museum telling the history of the great palace.

H My entire family hails from a suburb that, by its very name, still brings to mind past glories and that fateful evening. These days, Crystal Palace is just like any other busy commuter area, swallowed up by the greater London sprawl, but it used to be home to one of the largest glass structures in the world, the Crystal Palace.

You are going to read an extract from an article about science awards. For questions 44–53, choose from the sections (A–E) using the separate answer sheet. The sections may be selected more than once.

In which section are the following mentioned?

New awards could have a more significant impact if they were given to scientists who have a greater need for financial investment.	**44**	
Funding popular science communicators rather than prizes may be more worthwhile for society.	**45**	
The new science awards are backed by a different type of elite.	**46**	
Some scientists are unhappy about the unequal distribution of investment in science.	**47**	
Scientists are suspicious of the principles underlying the new science awards.	**48**	
New science awards have largely been funded by private rather than public enterprise.	**49**	
The system of awarding scientists for their discoveries has not kept pace with changing scientific practices.	**50**	
The impact that generous financial incentives will have on the direction of future research.	**51**	
The newer science awards are rooted in cooperation rather than individuality.	**52**	
The likelihood of prize-winning scientists needing substantial financial funding is low.	**53**	

The New Science Awards Redefining Success

A challenge to tradition, but not without their problems

A

For a little over a century, in a somewhat staid and dull ceremony in Stockholm in January, the Nobel prizes have been awarded to worthy scientists by the King of Sweden. But, as in all walks of life, times change and science awards are no different. The new awards or 'new Nobels', as they have been dubbed, are no longer the preserve of prestigious institutions like the Swedish Academy. Instead, they are paid for by celebrity CEOs such as Mark Zuckerberg and other tech millionaires, with multimillion-dollar prizes and ceremonies that are glamorous affairs reminiscent of the Oscars. And this is something that scientists generally tend not to view in a particularly positive light. British astronomer Martin Rees says that many scientists are undecided about the new awards. He believes that these more recent awards are steered towards showcasing the wealthy donors as much as the scientists themselves. He is not the only award cynic and others have joined him in voicing concerns, including American physicist Frank Wilczek who wonders about the virtues of awarding large prizes in the advancement of science.

B

There are indeed some serious concerns about all this. The most worrying of which centres around the world view and associated power of the funders, be they individuals like Zuckerberg or large global corporations. The problem is that these elite minorities are predominantly Western with a specific shared world view of the value of knowledge, as well as the aspects of science that are deserving of investment, be that time-based or financial. Many people are anxious that younger researchers trying to cut their teeth in a world where funding is increasingly competitive could easily adapt their research to the visions held by the funders of these new awards, visions which may or may not have the interests of humanity as a whole at their heart. Oversight is a key aspect of research in a way that it is not seen in business, especially the tech giants who prize innovation over all other things. This shift in the motivations of those who are the guardians of science awards should raise alarm bells for us all.

C

The Breakthrough Prize in Life Sciences is an excellent example of this. The list of donors reads like a who's-who of celebrity tech CEOs and the price tag attached to each prize is $3 million. Most winners are highly regarded scientists with glittering careers and enviable publishing records. These huge prizes tend to go to scientists who are already extremely well-funded, and it could easily be argued that they are the least in need of such exorbitant sums. Furthermore, if these new awards and their glamourous ceremonies are designed to bring a new breed of celebrity science to public attention, they may be wasting their time. A quick YouTube search will show that the world has plenty of celebrity scientists boasting millions of followers worldwide, such as Brian Cox or Michio Kaku. Funding that aims to bring science to the general public should probably be diverted to the people who have proven track records in engaging people in science.

D

Despite the scepticism surrounding these new science awards, benefits do exist. In order to present a fair and balanced analysis of the positive impacts of such awards, these benefits should be highlighted. In recent times a key criticism of the original Nobel prizes has been the fact that they do not fully represent the way in which science is carried out in modern times. Nowadays most scientific inventions and discoveries are collaborative. This means that they rely on the cooperation and shared knowledge and expertise of dozens of scientists working in cross-cultural teams across several academic communities around the globe, rather than individuals working in isolation. Since the Nobel prizes can only be awarded to three people each year, many hard-working scientists go unnoticed, receiving little or no recognition for their contributions to research and discoveries that simply could not have happened without them. Contrary to this system, the Breakthrough Prize and others have been designed to reward entire teams and are therefore much wider in their scope and inclusivity.

E

However, there is a danger that these prizes could be seen as paying lip service to the principles of inclusivity and diversity. Although there are some non-Western prizes such as the Tang Prize, awarded to those working in Asian institutions, most winning teams are located in Western nations, and global inclusivity remains a challenge. Scientists such as Bob O'Hara, who works at a research centre in Frankfurt, warn of the widening gap between the rich and poor among the scientific community. Instead of talking about awards and large financial prizes, he cites as a concern the funding allocated to the search for treatments and cures for the diseases of the rich, rather than those that are widespread amongst developing nations. Many scientists strongly believe that the West must not just be allowed to dominate and marginalise other nations that have much to offer in terms of knowledge and research potential. These glamorous new science awards are a prime example of how scientists in developing nations might be able to benefit from the prize money far more than their western counterparts might.

Name ______________________________ **Date** ______________

Part 5

Mark the appropriate answer.

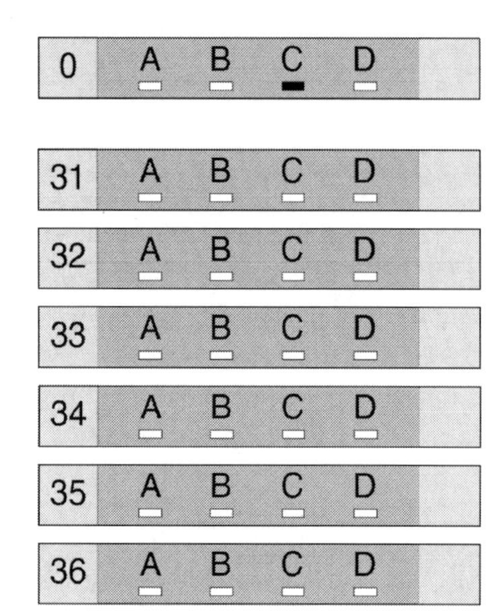

Part 6

Add the appropriate answer.

37	38	39	40	41	42	43

Part 7

Add the appropriate answer.

44	45
46	47
48	49
50	51
52	53

Cambridge C2 Proficiency
Reading: Parts 5–7

Test 2

You are going to read an extract from a textbook. For questions 31–36, mark the appropriate answer (A, B, C or D) that you think fits best according to the text.

Is Objective Reality a Myth?

It's easy to think that our visual experience or the fundamental concepts within society are objectively true, and there is good cause for this way of thinking to be desirable. It helps us to realise that we are not alone and have a shared experience, and it aids us in organising the abundance of information we receive as human beings. However, the idea of one objective reality is more debateable than you may think. Throughout history, shared beliefs have been disproved, and that we can perceive images moving on a television screen, when really it is a series of dots changing colour, indicates that visual perception can be deceiving.

Our shared realities, certainly in the modern Western world, are centred on material things that we can touch, the objectivity of science and humans, and our individual growth. Historian Greg Anderson claims that these principles are essentially an exception in the history of civilization. Before the Industrial Revolution, almost all western societies saw reality as quite a different set of concepts. Their worlds depended on things that today we might consider 'unreal', such as entities that control nature, and humans' lives were dictated by this. It was considered in the same way that we regard science today. In addition, many societies held little belief in 'the individual', as the individual was deemed inseparable from the family unit, which worked together as a whole to survive. And as these civilisations, in some form or other, continued in this way for several centuries, we should be sceptical that we, with our modern perception of life, know better.

However, reality is deeper than just a set of shared beliefs – reality is also a set of truths. The idea that there are 'known facts' and 'unknown facts' is something with which we all should probably reconcile ourselves in the modern world. Take the internet, for instance. While it is useful for looking up undisputed knowledge, for example that Paris is the capital of France, or that the Sun is our nearest star, there is also much more dubious information out there. This is evidenced in doctored photos or misrepresented figures that are placed online, and some people take this misinformation as fact, simply because they have blindly trusted it to be true, or because it has confirmed a belief that they already held.

Even our senses do not escape from this controversy surrounding an objective reality. One key example of this is the placebo effect, which not only occurs in medical or clinical trials, but in everyday situations too. Placebos – in other words medicines that appear to be a real but in reality aren't – are often used in clinical trials as a way to measure drug effects, yet sometimes patients' symptoms appear to improve when taking placebos and not the real drugs. Even our vision, as cognitive scientist Donald Hoffman explains, often misrepresents the truth to us because our brains have to make sense of the received visual data. He uses the example of a train to show how this works. We think we all know what a train is exactly, but physicists would tell you a train is merely a collection of moving particles, particles that we have given a label in order to attach shared, and indispensable, meanings to the object. Optical illusions provide yet further evidence of how our brains organise visuals to offer some kind of meaning that is essentially false. Such illusions include the Ponzo depth-perception illusion, in which two identical lines appear to be different sizes when viewed in conjunction with converging track lines going into the distance.

So, whatever our experience of the world, the signs are that it is filled with subjectivity in a way that perhaps we didn't quite imagine before. Science moves on and theories that once were taken as fact are disproved, our beliefs are subject to the modern world we live in and its values, the internet is littered with untruths, and our minds can play tricks on us. Therefore, to be as bold as to say 'our way is best' is perhaps a little conceited. We know as much as our brains allow and our physical context tells us.

31 In the first paragraph, what does the writer suggest about the human relationship with objective truth?

A It is something we subconsciously know is largely inaccurate.

B It helps us to construct common meaning from what we experience.

C It is a tool for bonding with other humans around us.

D It is hard for us to tell whether something is objectively real.

32 What does the article tell us about past views of common realities in paragraph 2?

A They were inaccurate.

B They slowly evolved.

C They had longevity.

D They became illogical.

33 In the third paragraph, how does the writer feel about information on the internet?

A We should attempt to establish the accuracy of information.

B We believe only what we choose to believe.

C We need to be less trusting of what we read.

D We should live with the varied quality of information.

34 The writer uses the placebo effect to show us:

A the limits of our senses.

B the benefits of thinking positively.

C the drawbacks of medical trials.

D the power of pure belief.

35 What does Donald Hoffman think about the way we interpret reality?

A It serves a purpose.

B It aids communication.

C It is a brain deficiency.

D It impedes our understanding.

36 How does the writer summarise their attitude to what we think is real?

A We need to try to understand the environment around us.

B We aren't as all-knowing as we deem ourselves to be.

C We still have a lot to learn about objective reality.

D We should give ourselves up to life's ambiguities.

You are going to read an extract from an article. Seven paragraphs have been removed. Select from the paragraphs (A–H) the one that fits each gap (37–43). There is one extra paragraph that you do not need to use.

The Reinvention of a Brand

Almost everyone knows what Lego is and has probably played with it at some point in their lives. Since the company's foundation in 1932, millions have been delighted by the interlocking bricks that can unleash the creative ideas lurking inside us, adults and children alike. Part of the attraction is in the attention to detail, which of course the customer is largely unaware of. The Danish creator, Ole Kirk Christiansen, was meticulous about 'doing things right', which is one of the reasons why this popular toy has stood the test of time.

37	

What led to this unfortunate state was a series of bad decisions based on advice given by external business consultants. At this time, product diversity and business expansion were very much in fashion in all sorts of different industries and so The Lego Group had started to move into various sectors that lay well outside its expertise. It had created theme parks, and clothes and jewellery for girls, none of which were creating significant revenues so it was clearly time to get back to basics and rethink their product strategy.

38	

This renewed focus chimed well with the company's motto, created by the founder, Christiansen, and which is carved into a plaque at the Lego Museum in Billund in Denmark: 'Only the best is good enough'. This idea of focusing on strengths and not expanding into unknown areas is a key feature of the thinking in Danish business culture, and the mentality of The Lego Group is that the company is about engineering good-quality products for play and that they should not stray from this focus.

39	

The change in the company's fortunes has been analysed extensively by business experts fascinated by such a momentous financial turnaround ever since. Countless books have been written about it and many other large brands have analysed The Lego Group's approach to see how it can help their businesses.

One of the fundamental approaches taken by the Danish company is based on forging partnerships that allow collaboration on innovative projects while at the same time remaining true to their principles of doing what they do best.

40	

One of the most successful of these was with NASA, the American space agency. The two organisations participated in a robotics competition during the 1990s, which was a big hit among the participants and the organisations' relationship has remained strong ever since. This is partly because The Lego Group is deeply interested in how children play and learn, and also because NASA has a long history of being involved in educational projects for young people. Both want to encourage children to develop an interest in science and engineering through fun.

41	

The Lego Group has never targeted its products on just one gender. However, historically, its popularity has been overwhelmingly enjoyed by boys. They love the mini figures of people and don't much care how realistic they are. Girls, on the other hand, need to be able to identify with model people. Apparently, this does not happen with the traditional figures, which is why, after several years of market research, a set of figures aimed at girls was developed.

42	

Focusing on what customers like and want has proven to be useful in a variety of ways. In what could be called one of the first attempts at crowd sourcing, The Lego Group got its fans and customers to vote on designs and even suggest ideas for new products. Ideas that went on to be commissioned earned 1% of sales for the people that had suggested them – a great way to build customer engagement.

43	

A A team from The Lego Group travels extensively and engages with children and parents to develop a better understanding of what kinds of toys children like and dislike. By observing children interacting with toys and each other, the company can target its products more effectively, which is how the team learned more about marketing to girls, a sector that had previously eluded them.

B Innovation has been key to maintaining customers' interest, too, as can be seen in the Lego movies and the adult architecture range, and also in the new kids' social media platform, which allows children too young to partake in other social networking platforms to share their designs safely online. These extensions into cinema, adult play and technology seem to represent the final pieces of a huge jigsaw puzzle for a complete learning and creativity system by one company.

C In order to do this, the newly appointed CEO set about rebuilding the organisation. Business operations were streamlined, and many things were scaled back such as staff and the product ranges. In addition, the company sold all the extras that were not a core part of the business, which meant that it was able to return to its roots.

D By returning to the original ethos, the company was able to put emphasis on renewed energy in the brand and become financially stable. Over a decade later the results were clear to see, and they were extremely positive. In 2017 the company was voted the number one toy brand in many countries. It reported sales of over £600 million that year, and the turnaround was seen as amazing, one of the most impressive success stories in commercial history.

E This rethink led to moving the company's factories to alternative locations. Many large corporations outsource their production operations to parts of the world offering lower labour costs, but The Lego Group has factories in Europe, South America and Asia so that a wide range of products can be quickly shipped to their key markets to keep their customers, both adults and children, happy.

F However, this hasn't always been the case. Despite its huge success during the 1970s and 80s, by the beginning of the twenty-first century, the company's fortunes were looking decidedly precarious. It was in debt to the tune of $800 million, and sales were in fast decline. What had seemed inconceivable throughout the company's history, a total and utter collapse was beginning to look like reality.

G The company became extremely successful and sales skyrocketed in a short space of time. This attention to detail shows how serious The Lego Group is about understanding play. In fact, the company thinks that it is important enough to have set up a sister company to study child development as well as partnering with the children's charity UNICEF and financing the first Professor of Play at Cambridge University in the UK.

H In recent years The Lego Group has worked with quite a diverse set of companies in order to innovate, and an example of this is the collaboration with Lucasfilm, the production company behind the Star Wars films. In 1999 the *Lego Star Wars* franchise was launched at a toy fair in New York and it became instantly popular. The partnership worked well for both companies and paved the way for further innovative Lego Group partnerships.

You are going to read an article on travel adventures. For questions 44–53, select the travel writer (A–E) using the separate answer sheet. Each travel writer may be selected more than once.

Which travel writer:

says their luck initially changed for the worse?	**44**	
had some rather stereotypical opinions?	**45**	
got to experience a different kind of life?	**46**	
learned not to jump to conclusions?	**47**	
has had a lot of travel problems in the past?	**48**	
caused a fuss about something?	**49**	
felt like they were the odd one out?	**50**	
was reliant on another person?	**51**	
was in awe of their surroundings?	**52**	
thought they were ready for anything?	**53**	

Far-flung Adventures

Isla Perkins speaks to five travel writers to discover their most memorable travel experience

A Ethan Simmons

I've been on a fair few trips, not all of them easy, but when I think back to one trip that really stands out for me, it has to be my overnight adventure in the depths of the jungle. It was probably a memorable experience for numerous reasons, not least because it tested my courage! Fortunately, and crucially, a guide was at our disposal to deal with any eventualities that might occur or, at least, keep us alive! I felt completely at his mercy and, undoubtedly, we'd have been toast if it hadn't been for him. Of those memorable 36 hours, the highlights included being bitten by fire ants and chased by a monkey, and to top it off, we slept amongst it all, albeit with one eye open! My overwhelming recollection, though, is what a feast for my senses the jungle was – at night it is like an orchestra of the natural world.

B Ruth Gonzalez

My most memorable experience occurred when I was a fearless teen on a long-distance bus, travelling solo with a little cash in my bag and my bank card in my sock for safekeeping. However, during the journey I had the paralysing realisation that my sock felt suspiciously light, and a panicked fumble through my belongings confirmed what I'd dreaded – my card was nowhere to be seen. The fear spread through me, and before I knew it I'd burst into tears, making quite a scene that all the passengers witnessed! It was at this point I became aware of a suspicious-looking woman, stealing hidden glances at me and whispering to someone on her mobile in a language I didn't understand. The horror continued when I alighted, and she grabbed my wrist and started dragging me towards a strange man! However, contrary to my rather dark suspicions, the man told me his mother was worried about me but spoke no English, and they proceeded to go out of their way to make sure I was safe and calm, even taking me to the Embassy! Perhaps I should be more trusting in the future.

C Matt Cooper

I've been at the mercy of a whole host of airline hassles when travelling, but none was more memorable than the flight complications I had over my 21st birthday. I was returning from Australia to the UK, but blizzards had caused havoc in the UK leading to a standstill for most flights bound that way. I truly felt I'd won the lottery when they announced that we could take off, but little did I know we'd be stuck on the tarmac at our refuelling point in Bangkok, the city that indirectly played host to my birthday. I passed the time with four strangers on the plane, all of whom were travelling solo like me, and it was one of the most rewarding moments of my life as we came together from four different corners of the world to communicate in the little shared English that we had, and to form friendships that are still lasting to this day. And the most priceless part of all? I married one of them!

D Taisa Vasilyev

I used to treat people who took two weeks to go and lay on a beach with contempt, considering them to be unadventurous and uncultured, but my recent trek across the Grand Canyon, world-famous for its jaw-dropping landscape, has made me think twice. I'd decided to go it alone, and while on a deserted path, teetering on a rock trying to get some shots of an eagle circling in the sky, I slipped and ended up with my foot jammed between two rocks. After some wriggling around I realised that it was stuck fast. Of course, as a seasoned adventurer I was prepared for such eventualities and so grabbed my mobile to call for help, only to see I had no reception. That will teach me for going off the beaten track! I had no choice but to spend the night out there on the rocks, waiting for help and imagining the worst, until a couple came past early next morning. In the future, I think I'll stick to an all-inclusive hotel!

E Teresa Small

I was inter-railing around Europe, and it was great, if nothing out of the ordinary, at least until I got to Greece. From the moment I alighted from the train in Athens I noticed a different air around me. I wondered if it was paranoia, but I got the sense that people were giving me furtive glances, and I noticed hushed whispers that I suspected were made in my direction. I couldn't put my finger on it exactly, but I had a hunch that something wasn't right, and that I was at the centre of it. I spent a good half day feeling like that until I got on a boat to Naxos and someone asked me for an autograph. They say everyone has a double and it turns out mine is a famous Greek soap opera star! Once I realised this, I revelled in the attention, causing a stir wherever I went and even signing the odd autograph, even though I wasn't the real deal! After all, who doesn't want to feel special once in a while?

Cambridge C2 Proficiency Reading — Answer sheet

Name ______________________ **Date** ____________

Part 5

Mark the appropriate answer.

0	A	B	C ▬	D
31	A	B	C	D
32	A	B	C	D
33	A	B	C	D
34	A	B	C	D
35	A	B	C	D
36	A	B	C	D

Part 6

Add the appropriate answer.

37	38	39	40	41	42	43

Part 7

Add the appropriate answer.

44	45
46	47
48	49
50	51
52	53

Cambridge C2 Proficiency Reading: Parts 5–7

Test 3

You are going to read an extract from a travel memoir. For questions 31–36, mark the appropriate answer (A, B, C or D) that you think fits best according to the text.

Journal of a Reluctant Traveller

The journey to Santa Cruz was uneventful, which I was grateful for. I'd really not wanted to get stranded halfway up a mountain in the dark like what happened a couple of weeks ago, coming across the border from Chile into Bolivia. Even then I knew that choosing the most inexpensive bus company was risky, but their bus was scheduled to depart immediately and I'd been impatient yet again. A few hours later, when the bus started belching out smoke and shuddered to a halt, I was furious with myself. Of course, by then it was too late and so I spent an uncomfortable night wondering whether I'd be stranded there forever.

Anyway, I'd learned that lesson the hard way and decided that this time I'd treat myself to one of the modern tour buses with reclining seats, which was obviously well worth the investment of an extra twenty dollars. Also, I was determined not to allow that horrific journey to get to me too much since travel was supposed to be an adventure, after all, and not everything could go smoothly. That was the reason for this trip in the first place. I was supposed to be growing as a person and apparently the freedom of traveling in unknown places would allow me to discover things about myself that had lain hidden in my overly stressful London lifestyle.

Initially, I'd been suspicious of this as my self-image was strongly aligned with the discipline needed for a high-flying career as a tax advisor to multinational corporations, not some wandering hippie with dreams of rescuing dolphins. Why I imagined that disconnecting from the relentless pressures of my life wouldn't be positive I have no idea, but in the weeks leading up to my holiday I'd told anyone willing to listen that I disputed the fact that travel could be transformational.

A glance through my journal, however, would quickly demonstrate my ignorance of the power of travel. As the weeks passed, my entries began to take on a different vibe, from the first ones itemising facts like they were a list of groceries to more descriptive pieces with observations and a gradual emergence of emotive responses to the world around me. It was like a role reversal because, while previously the world had existed to serve my needs, I now felt a responsibility to be connected to my surroundings. And that morning, as I hopped off the luxury bus, it occurred to me that I felt rested and calm in a way in which I hadn't really understood before.

I spotted a café in the corner of the square, sat down at a shady table outside and, while sipping my coffee, noticed the server as she happily bustled around, greeting all the customers, chatting and laughing as she went, and it occurred to me that I couldn't recall the last time I'd had fun at work. Anyway, when returning from the bathroom, a sign with 'Help!' scrawled in large letters next to the tourist leaflets caught my eye and I leaned over to inspect the typed information underneath. 'Manager needed for 6 months. Must have English and Spanish. Speak to Sofia.'

Sofia, the server from earlier, had seen me looking at the notice and rushed over. Not long after this, the whole story about how her mother had just undergone major surgery and so she was going to have to return home and nurse her through the recovery came out. Apparently, home was some distance away, on the other side of the country, and she hadn't yet found anyone to manage the café in her absence. "The problem is that I do everything so I need someone trustworthy, someone who understands figures and can manage the business not just serve coffee to tourists," she said. And at that moment, right there in the café, I realised that the proposition was too tempting to resist.

Sofia spent the evening explaining how the payment machine and bookkeeping software worked, and it all seemed fairly straightforward. The next morning, she handed me the keys and her phone number on a scrap of paper, hugged me and disappeared. As I somewhat nervously stepped into the sunshine to greet my first customers, I tried to picture my office and flat back in London and noticed that the images seemed to be fading just a little around the edges.

31 What does the writer say about the bus journeys on her trip?

A Any adverse experiences were due to her own decision-making.

B The overnight trips were more draining than she expected.

C She was annoyed that the buses were in an such a neglected state.

D They kept to the scheduled departure times surprisingly well.

32 On the subject of traveling, the writer suggests that she:

A is as a veteran, constantly in search of adventures.

B only enjoys traveling when there are no incidents.

C prefers to splash out on luxury holidays closer to home.

D feels that she should broaden her horizons.

33 Before setting off on her trip, the writer:

A was convinced of the healing powers of travel.

B hoped that it would live up to her expectations.

C was sceptical of its life-changing potential.

D believed that it would be the key to all her troubles.

34 How does the writer's account of her travels change over time?

A She starts to record her experiences more accurately.

B Her journal becomes more reflective and thoughtful.

C The more she travels, the less she feels compelled to write.

D It better reflects her understanding of the local cultures.

35 The writer implies that she accepted the job in the café because:

A she suspected it might benefit her mental health.

B her linguistic abilities matched the requirements.

C she felt sorry for Sofia's plight and wanted to help.

D her employment experience was identical.

36 What is the overall effect that travelling has had on the writer?

A Her personality has become more outgoing.

B It has enhanced her practical life skills.

C It has made her reconsider her life goals.

D She regrets her previous life.

You are going to read an extract from an article. Seven paragraphs have been removed. Select from the paragraphs (A–H) the one that fits each gap (37–43). There is one extra paragraph that you do not need to use.

A Clothing Revolution

If you're bored with your wardrobe and are looking for a new style, you might want to think about one of the latest trends in fashion, and that is digital clothing. Unlike all other fashion trends in the past, digital fashion is unique insofar as it does not actually exist. In this brave new world clothes are made from pixels rather than fabric and customers can be far more imaginative; in fact, the sky is the limit when it comes to designs in the digital arena.

37	

However, it is worth bearing in mind that this type of online image manipulation is not a new idea. People have always paid attention to their profile pictures on a variety of online platforms that they use in both their private and professional lives. In the same way that appearance can be influential in real life, our digital appearance plays an important role in how we are perceived by others, which means people pay attention to it. What is new, though, is the growing number of advantages of digital over physical fashion.

38	

By only producing a digital version of an item of clothing at first, the costs that are associated with making samples, having face-to-face meetings and other logistical concerns can be drastically reduced. The designers can work on each item of clothing using technology rather than having to produce countless physical items during the design process. Improvements in technology have meant that seeing a physical garment is not as essential as it used to be.

39	

This is likely to become more important in the near future as companies rush to meet consumers' needs. Already it is clear that fashion brands are adapting their collections to meet the demands of new lifestyles, many of which are becoming more flexible in terms of working arrangements. As more people work from home and attitudes towards formal office attire shift, the fashion industry will need to continue to respond and create new types of clothing that allow for more comfort and ease of movement as opposed to stiff formal wear.

40	

They could also start asking for a garment to be copied using different material as a way of developing a unique personal wardrobe. Many designers are already way ahead of consumers in this regard and are experimenting with new materials or new ways of using existing materials. Some current suggestions include clothing that is made entirely from small lights or metal, or even from plants and flowers. The possibilities for creativity are endless and customers could end up with the clothes that they have always dreamed of owning yet could never find.

41	

Despite this being a huge step in the right direction, it is unlikely that attitudes to fashion and gender will change overnight as the technology is not quite as advanced as people might think. While many brands have an online fitting room for customers to try out clothes before they buy them, the body shapes used by this kind of software are fairly generic and still based on traditional views of male and female bodies that rarely conform to reality.

42	

As a result, digital clothing remains quite expensive, but this will change as the technology improves, and the video game sector can shed some light on customer engagement with digital fashion. For years, video game enthusiasts have been changing the appearance of their avatars through outfits and weapons, and are clearly happy to pay for this service, which has caused the costs of avatar clothing to fall as demand has increased.

43	

A While some of the new trends have started to emerge, such as the rise in demand for leisurewear, it is still unclear how the digital fashion market will develop. However, what is obvious it that it allows for self-expression in a far more nuanced way. For example, a customer only needs to buy one digital t-shirt, but they could change the image or slogan on that one t-shirt for many different versions.

B No one knows whether the cost of digital clothing will come down in a few years' time. At present, the market appears to be growing, but some designers have suggested that it is just a passing phase and its popularity could disappear in a flash. As such they are cautious about investing time or money in something that may be around for just a few years.

C Personalisation and creating an individual look contribute to being a key part of the modern approach to identity, and we can do this by wearing original clothing in both the real and unreal worlds. The fact that people already do this with imaginary online characters means that it should come as no surprise that there is a growing desire to do the same with our online selves too.

D Costs can be decreased further through the reduction in the time to transport the products to both bricks-and-mortar-stores and online shopping platforms. This will enable companies to become more agile, to respond to consumers' needs and potentially to create more collections that will start to address individual lifestyle needs instead of being based around the four seasons.

E In contrast, the process of having clothing fitted to a specific body shape in a customer's photo is much more involved. Currently, this work is done by people and it is still quite a time-consuming process. Typically, clients upload a photograph and then this image is digitally dressed by using 3D-modelling software. From start to finish this process can take up to a whole working day.

F The most obvious of these is its sustainability. Given that that fashion industry is responsible for around 10% of greenhouse-gas emissions, there is a clear case for the sustainability of digital fashion. It can reduce waste considerably, both in terms of making the physical product, but also by reducing the carbon footprint of the design process, something that people generally think about far less.

G Fashion designers have much more freedom with digital garments and can play around in more creative ways to make clothing more customisable and individual. All this has become possible because people have been prepared for digital fashion by a social-media-driven, modern society that is obsessed with photos and online images.

H By putting the individual at the heart of digital fashion, there is also the opportunity for a less prescriptive approach to clothing for men and women. For many years the fashion industry has been criticised for using thin models and causing body-image issues among young people. Because digital fashion can be so unique, it challenges these ideas.

You are going to read an extract from an article on muscles in the human body. For questions 44–53, choose from the sections (A–F) using the separate answer sheet. The sections may be selected more than once.

In which section are the following mentioned?

A connection between muscles and how humans combat cold climates has been found.	**44**	
A change in environment is highly likely to have been the trigger for the genetic alteration.	**45**	
Studies of talented athletes are helping scientists answer an age-old question.	**46**	
New medicines have come out of combining research fields.	**47**	
The proportion of muscle types in humans remains the same irrespective of physical training.	**48**	
People lacking the protein might be less able to maintain a healthy lifestyle.	**49**	
Slow-twitch muscles are better for regulating body temperature.	**50**	
Sporting excellence is due to the biological makeup of an individual.	**51**	
A higher proportion of slow-twitch muscles may cause mobility problems for some people.	**52**	
Treatment could become more precisely targeted as a result of muscle research.	**53**	

Answering Old and New Questions in Science

Understanding more about the muscles in the human body

A

For a long time, scientists have wondered why some people are better than others at tolerating the cold, and recent research into why athletes from different parts of the globe excel in different sports may have shed some light on the issue. Athletes from certain countries are supremely successful long-distance runners and frequently beat all other competitors in global competitions such the Olympics, while athletes who perform exceptionally well in sports that require short bursts of energy often come from completely different parts of the world. Research now suggests that athletes can be categorised by muscle types. The human body has fast-twitch and slow-twitch muscles, the word 'twitch' referring to the movement of the muscles, and, according to scientists, both muscle types function differently. Fast-twitch muscles contract quickly and are used for actions such as jumping and sprinting, whereas slow-twitch muscles are the opposite and are used for slower actions such as walking or jogging.

B

Humans have different combinations of these two muscle types that are set at birth and cannot be changed through exercise, which accounts for why some people are naturally good at specific sports compared to others. Athletes who possess more fast-twitch muscles will always have a competitive edge in sports where speed is a decisive factor, and this is also true for long-distance running where those who have more slow-twitch muscles will be more likely to win races. What is interesting is that in both cases the presence of one of these muscle types is much higher in people who end up becoming athletes, where the ratio of fast-twitch and slow-twitch muscles is disproportionate compared to the rest of the population, where it is about 50:50. In essence, then, these people are born to be athletes.

C

What makes these muscles different is the presence of a specific protein that appears in the fast-twitch muscles and has therefore been labelled as the 'gene for speed'. The discovery of this protein has also contributed to ongoing research over the last decade into the ability of humans to tolerate cold climates. Researchers have observed that this protein, which is present in fast-twitch muscles, is part of this phenomenon because when human beings are cold these muscles contract repeatedly and quickly, which explains why people shiver when they are exposed to lower temperatures. All of these tiny muscle movements create heat and that is how people warm up their bodies.

D

However, one in five people in the world lack this protein and so do not shiver or warm themselves with their fast-twitch muscles. Instead, they use their slow-twitch muscles, which are more efficient and allow people to tolerate colder temperatures for longer periods of time.

The reason why so many people do not have this protein is down to evolution. As homo sapiens began to move north from Africa over 40,000 years ago they would have started to settle in colder climates, and this would have caused a change in their metabolisms in order to manage living in these new conditions. Scientists suggest that a gene most likely mutated during this transition, causing the loss of this protein, the evolutionary result of which was that people shivered less in the cold thus preserving energy.

E

This research into muscles could prove useful for scientists and doctors working in certain areas of healthcare, one of which being the treatment of muscle-wasting diseases. These diseases are commonly inherited, and it could be interesting to see how people with and without this protein respond to different kinds of medical interventions over time. One study found that there is a connection between this 'gene for speed' and how long it takes for some muscle-wasting diseases to progress and so, based on this finding, scientists may be able to develop medication that is more effective for different groups of patients. Another key area is in that of obesity, which is one of the most concerning diseases of the modern world affecting millions of people in many cultures. If people without the specific protein are able to maintain their body temperatures more easily, this suggest that, unless they follow a healthy diet and exercise regularly, the risk of obesity and associated problems such as diabetes may be considerably higher for them. It has been suggested that this information could be beneficial for doctors when advising patients on how to tackle obesity.

F

Finally, researchers have also noted that people with more slow- than fast-twitch muscles (in other words, those with the gene mutation and therefore without the protein) may injure themselves more frequently and easily as they get older. Given that fast-twitch muscles handle explosive movements such as falling, it follows that older people who do not have as many fast-twitch muscles may be more susceptible to accidents. The research that set out to answer the age-old question as to why certain people are able to tolerate the cold more than others has, like many scientific enquiries, provided innovation in medicine by incorporating studies into a much newer field, that of sports science.

Name ______________________ Date ____________

Part 5

Mark the appropriate answer.

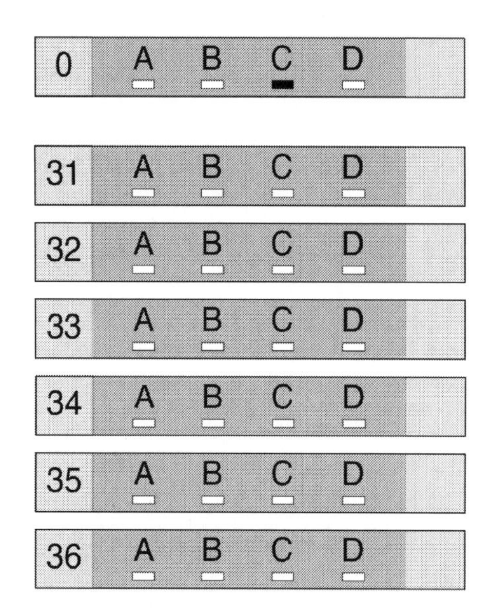

Part 6

Add the appropriate answer.

37	38	39	40	41	42	43

Part 7

Add the appropriate answer.

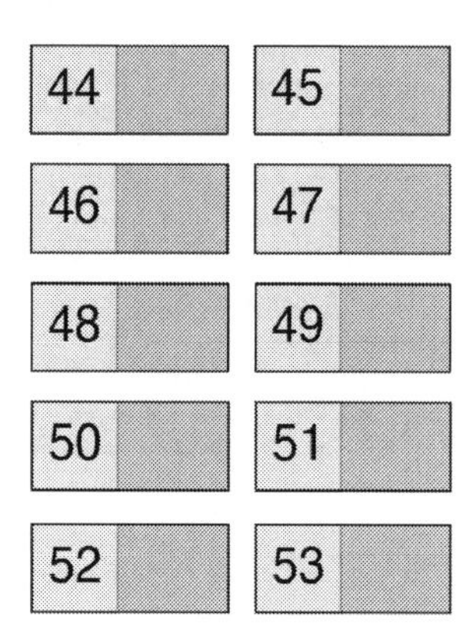

Cambridge C2 Proficiency
Reading: Parts 5–7

Test 4

You are going to read an article about horror. For questions 31–36, mark the appropriate answer (A, B, C or D) that you think fits best according to the text.

The Lure of Horror

If, like me, you've ever spent an evening hidden behind your cushion anticipating the climax to some petrifying scene in a film, you're among millions of others who can't help but watch horror films without the faintest idea of why they're putting themselves through such an ordeal. Of course, there are some people who watch such films to come across as fearless, even if underneath their bold exterior they are filled with terror, but there are also huge numbers of viewers who truly relish a good scare.

The reasons for differing reactions to horror may be down to how people's brains function. Watching these kinds of movies releases chemicals such as adrenaline, endorphins and dopamine, which make most people feel charged with energy, mirroring the 'fight or flight' energy rush we experience in times of peril, and, coupled with the safe environment in which we usually watch these types of movies, we end up with a physical fear response that we know is no actual threat to our safety. Due to these chemicals, we can also get a feeling of pride once we've endured the entire film, as if we've confronted the horror ourselves!

Horror films also appeal to our sense of 'what if', and exploring these kinds of scenarios aids us in forward-planning for disasters. As ridiculous as it sounds, when we watch films presenting characters in dire straits (when, for example, someone is trapped in a cave or running from a baddie), we naturally set about contemplating how we would react if we were in the shoes of those in danger on screen. This reaction is a subconscious way in which we prepare for the worst and reflect on how we would handle such menaces, and by opening ourselves up to a variety of traumatising events on film, it can make coping with unpleasant, albeit less dramatic, real-life situations easier. After all, it's never going to get as bad as a zombie apocalypse, hopefully!

Watching these kinds of films also offers us a sense of mental superiority to others as we believe that we could avert most of the disasters that befall the characters. Let's face it, many characters in horror films make disastrous choices: How often have you been watching a movie and screamed for the heroine not to go back into the house or into the basement? These formulaic movies enable us to conclude that we could never find ourselves in such a disastrous situation, because we would be far more wary than the short-sighted sap we see on the screen, and, as a result, we gain confidence in our own abilities. Further to making us feel clever, these films also provide a form of bonding opportunity for many people. Only the most dedicated horror fans watch these films alone in the dead of night; most of us watch them while clutching hold of others around us, and this is simply because the experience of being afraid and shocked connects us to our fellow viewers.

You probably have a friendship group that includes a combination of people who either love or loathe horror, and we shouldn't judge the reactions of others in terms of this genre. After all, we know that horror is more about how the chemicals in our brains are reacting rather than our own sense of bravery. Some people also have a better ability to suspend belief than others, which might heighten their chemical reactions. People who enjoy horror and the feeling of being scared are often well aware that what they are witnessing is fake and just an improbable diversion, but those who tend to get wrapped up in the story (and take a leap of faith to believe that these things could really happen) can find such films unbearable.

However, perhaps if you're determined to enjoy a horror film with someone who traditionally isn't a horror lover, there is an answer. Horror seems terrifying until you look at it from a broader perspective. How many times have you seen the baddie pounce from behind a curtain in the dead of night? It might seem terrifying at first, but that baddie would have had to be standing behind that curtain for who knows how many hours waiting for the victim to casually pass. They probably got caught in the curtain themselves, and almost definitely had cramp by the time their victim turned up. Sometimes, asking the most pragmatic questions makes a horror film turn into a joke.

31 In the first paragraph, what is the writer's reaction to horror films?

A They try to avoid watching any of them.

B They have a love-hate relationship with them.

C They enjoy the feeling of fear experienced.

D They find them a terrifying ordeal.

32 In paragraph two, the writer cites that horror films can give us a sense of:

A insecurity.

B anticipation.

C misadventure.

D accomplishment.

33 What does the writer find 'ridiculous' in paragraph three?

A How we imagine ourselves as the characters.

B How we react to certain plots in horror films.

C How some characters react to situations.

D How we compare horror films to real-life scenarios.

34 What is the writer's perspective on most horror film victims?

A They can't see the danger.

B They have limited abilities.

C They are predictably dim.

D They are stereotypical.

35 In the fifth paragraph, the writer suggests horror films scare people who:

A are more realistic than others.

B are receptive to the story.

C have negative beliefs.

D see themselves as emotional.

36 What advice does the writer give at the end?

A Think of why the villain is doing it.

B Realise how improbable the story is.

C Laugh at the ridiculous storylines.

D Watch horror films from a more practical angle.

You are going to read an extract from a magazine article on authorship. Seven paragraphs have been removed. Select from the paragraphs (A–H) the one that fits each gap (37–43). There is one extra paragraph that you do not need to use.

How I Became a Writer

Glancing at the author's copy of the book on the desk beside me, I smile inwardly and resume typing the email to my editor. I am confirming the arrangements for one of the promotional events scheduled for my new book. I'm particularly satisfied with how this, my fourth non-fiction work on art, has turned out and Zandra, my editor, has been especially complimentary too, saying it demonstrates my overall development as a writer.

37

Given all that, it seems strange that I find myself here, but for some people life is full of twists and turns, and this is definitely true for me. My teenage years were spent dabbling in writing for the school magazine, not with any particularly lofty ambitions of turning it into a career, but instead an interest in crafting well-written pieces and a vague idea of perhaps being published one day.

38

When I compare it to those of my contemporaries, my experience seems extraordinary nowadays. With the internet having transformed the industry, it's hard to imagine how writers managed to get any work prior to its invention, but of course the truth is that there just weren't that many of them. Fast-forward to the modern age and everyone seems to be a blogger or in the process of self-publishing their novel.

39

One evening I got a call from her to say that she was struggling with the text for an upcoming exhibition brochure and could I give her a hand, or at least some guidance. Apparently, the text to accompany her artwork was supposed to be quite formal, and she was having difficulty finding the right tone. I warned her not to have very high expectations, but said that I'd give it a try, nonetheless. Later that evening I managed to produce something I thought would be deemed acceptable and emailed it to her.

40

Having been impressed by my piece describing the exhibition in their brochure, she managed to track me down, first through contacting the gallery and then my sister, and that is how I ended up nearly choking on my coffee one morning while reading an email requesting me to write a series of articles to support the summer season of local artists' exhibitions. To my amusement, she apologised for the low fee, but suggested that further, more lucrative commissions could follow if this one were to be successful.

41

But this was her world – artists were accustomed to sourcing work by networking, whereas I had no previous experience of this kind of thing and confessed that I was extremely uneasy about it all. After weighing up all the advantages and disadvantages, Louisa persuaded me to take the plunge, and to my surprise, that is exactly what I did, firing off an acceptance email that afternoon before I had the opportunity to change my mind again.

42

After that first summer, I was hooked on writing and started wondering whether I could change career. I was in my fifties and concerned about giving up my job security, yet I couldn't stop thinking that writing, as I found it so enjoyable and satisfying, was what I should be doing. The magazine had given me an editor, Zandra, who had managed to find me some more commissions and, as promised, the payments did become considerably higher and I was starting to feel like I could make a living from my writing after all.

43

A This developed into a stronger desire for recognition, and, as an aspiring writer, I'd spend months handwriting or, later, typing out manuscripts, sending them off to magazines and publishers and anxiously awaiting responses that often never came. In a strange twist of fate, however, my entrance to the literary world would come through an altogether more un-conventional route.

B I actually started writing fairly late in life, after working for the local council for many years. As far as work was concerned, I definitely didn't want to be in the limelight. Although I was into literature, it was predominantly for personal enjoyment because although I admit that I always wanted acknowledgement for my writing, I hadn't the slightest desire to be famous.

C As my readership grew, so did my reputation as a writer and before long I was writing articles for other print and digital magazines, as well as for galleries. A book deal followed a few years later and by that time I had established myself as a credible art writer, and while it's unrealistic to expect the books I write to appear on a bestseller list, I make enough to live well and every day I am grateful for my writing career.

D Well, to be honest I didn't know what to think and the prospect of having to write something to a standard and when payment was involved filled me with terror. Questions came flooding through my mind and I immediately messaged my sister demanding an urgent meeting, during which she strongly advised me to seize the opportunity.

E My first attempt was a disaster because I just couldn't find the right words to describe with any depth of feeling the exhibition paintings that were right in front of my eyes. I was trying too hard to impress instead of writing from the heart to bring the paintings to life for someone without a background in art appreciation.

F It was a real success and I was delighted to have taken part. However, I had no idea that this would set the wheels in motion to entirely change my life. Little did anyone know, but one of guests at the opening night was a woman called Rebecca Martin who worked for the online arts magazine, *Palette*.

G Over the following months I devoted every spare moment of my time to attending exhibitions and crafting articles on the merits and demerits of the region's aspiring artists. I have to admit that the whole thing was thrilling; my brain was constantly buzzing with ideas, and I enjoyed watching them take shape as I happily typed into the night on my laptop.

H In addition to my interest in books, I have always had a passion for art, especially impressionism. Wandering around galleries is an absolute pleasure for me, although I don't have an artistic bone in my body, unlike my sister, Louisa, who is remarkably talented. And by that, I mean she has managed to forge a career as an artist rather than it just being a hobby.

You are going to read an extract from a textbook. For questions 44–53, select the expert (A–D) using the separate answer sheet. The expert may be selected more than once.

In which sections are the following mentioned?

Switching to a plant that is easier to cultivate.	**44**
Producers are calling for a more responsible attitude to production.	**45**
People are often unaware of the importance of rubber in manufacturing.	**46**
The livelihoods of rubber producers are insecure.	**47**
The importance of reducing dependence on rubber from overseas.	**48**
The mass planting of rubber trees is seen as a controversial practice.	**49**
A well-founded fear is that the world's rubber trees could easily be destroyed.	**50**
The rubber production process is different to that of other natural materials.	**51**
The use of biological methods to increase the cultivation of a range of options.	**52**
Plants that could be cost-effective rubber replacements.	**53**

The Search for a New Wonder Material

As the world's supply of rubber becomes less reliable, a solution must be found

A

When people are asked to identify the materials that are indispensable to modern life, the one that springs to mind most often is plastic. Make this question about a naturally occurring material and the responses are more varied, ranging from wood to iron to coal. Yet the raw material that we rely on most for such products as medical equipment, clothing and vehicles tyres is of course rubber. It has an impressive range of properties, such as being waterproof, durable and flexible, and these properties are unique and cannot be made using synthetic materials. This is especially true when it comes to making tires for vehicles and airplanes. Unfortunately, the state of global rubber production is currently under threat due to disease, climate change and economics. Although the extraction of many other raw materials such as stone or timber is done via large corporations on an industrial scale, this is not the case with rubber. In fact, quite the opposite is true as approximately 85% of global rubber production is carried out by farmers with small plots of land in the forests of southeast Asia. It just so happens that there are millions of people working the land in this way and therefore they are able to fulfil the supply of rubber required to help our lives run smoothly.

B

However, the price of rubber is not determined by the usual economic principle of supply and demand. Surprisingly, it is controlled by a financial market in Shanghai in much the same way as other commodities such as gold and oil, with traders making the price move up or down through buying and selling stocks and shares. This means that small farmers are at the mercy of these price fluctuations, and many of them cannot continue when prices are kept low for long periods of time. From their perspective, they are better off growing oil palms because palm oil is less labour intensive to produce than rubber. Even if prices were to rise enough to make rubber plantations consistently profitable, it is not as simple as that. There are those who argue that more rubber trees should be planted so that rising demand can be met, but the counterargument is that rubber trees have contributed just as significantly to the loss of biodiversity in Asia as oil palm plantations have. Governments in some countries have cleared vast areas of forest to grow rubber trees for profit alone, and there is a strong view that this kind of behaviour should not be encouraged. In fact, the majority of people believe that governments should lead the way in solving such problems of biodiversity.

C

In order to try to address the precarious conditions of both the environment and small farmers, many large rubber buyers, including the world's largest tire companies, have signed up to an organisation campaigning for sustainable rubber. It prohibits buying rubber from deforested land and aims to send a clear message to governments that clarifies what corporations are not prepared to accept. Other people in the industry are trying to promote the idea of a minimum price for rubber, similar to the Fair-Trade concept for coffee and cocoa, which aims to help small farmers stay in business. Besides these issues, the rubber tree also faces the constant threat of disease. Native to the Brazilian rainforest, the plant was wiped out there by a disease during the 1930s and now only grows in southeast Asia. Some scientists believe that with the amount of goods and people constantly traversing the world, it is only a matter of time before this disease arrives in Asia too. If this happens, the world's supply of rubber could vanish almost overnight and there is little that can be done to prevent such a disaster. This is worrying enough to have caused the European Union to add rubber to its list of critical raw materials.

D

All this has led scientists and commercial manufacturers to investigate alternative options, and there are a couple of plants that could potentially be used as substitutes. The most financially viable of these is guayule, a bush-like plant native to the USA and Mexico. One of the drivers behind the commercialisation of this plant is the fact that it grows in the USA, a country that currently relies heavily on the Asian rubber supply and which is actively looking for ways to reduce this reliance given the issues mentioned above. The US government previously experimented with guayule during the Second World War when rubber was scarce, but later abandoned the project when global trade got going again and Asian rubber became more readily available. Now, however, there are a few companies investing heavily in trying to make guayule an alternative, and there are signs that it could actually be successful. Researchers are working on breeding strains of the plant that could be grown on a much larger scale so as to avoid the current world reliance on a plant whose future is far from secure.

Name ______________________ Date ____________

Part 5

Mark the appropriate answer.

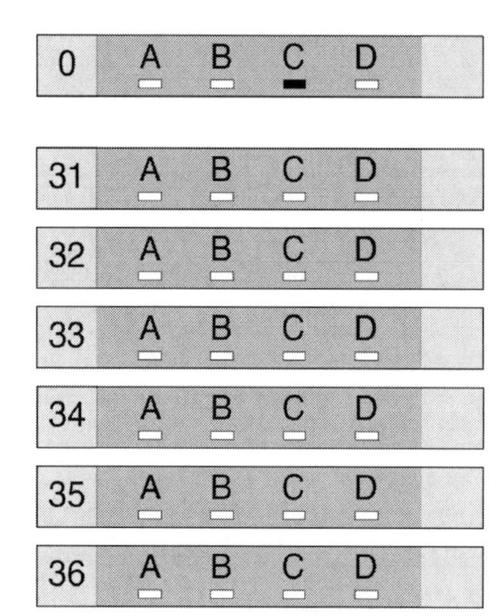

Part 6

Add the appropriate answer.

37	38	39	40	41	42	43

Part 7

Add the appropriate answer.

44	45
46	47
48	49
50	51
52	53

Cambridge C2 Proficiency
Reading: Parts 5–7

Test 5

You are going to read an extract from an article. For questions 31–36, mark the appropriate answer (A, B, C or D) that you think fits best according to the text.

Keeping Up With Innovation In Management

Until recently, had you asked the average employee of a medium-to-large company about their career aspirations, you would certainly have heard many state that management was their goal – not necessarily senior management but middle management, those roles in which people are responsible for a team by overseeing projects, monitoring performance and reporting upwards. Over the last fifty years or so, as companies grew so did the number of managerial roles and their attraction. Not anymore, though, if recent career-progression surveys are to be believed. A survey in 2019 reported that considerably less than half of the thousand employees interviewed across five countries saw management as a desirable career path.

It seems that management is undergoing some fairly radical changes, and for a more thorough understand of these contemporary developments it is worth taking a moment to step back in time to explore how management as a concept arose and persisted. Two monumental changes in the world reshaped *who does what and how* in the workplace. The first was driven by the machines of the Industrial Revolution that automated the skills of craftsmen and women whose dedication and resulting skills had previously been highly respected. Conversely, the new, less skilled workers had little demanded of them, except to follow orders precisely, and this gave rise to the role of 'manager' since the character of this workforce was often ill equipped for the nature of factory work, which resulted in frequent absences and accidents.

Now, the Age of Technology is making sweeping changes across the economy, and, ironically, this may be causing a return to the old ways of working. Technology is more than capable of doing many of the activities associated with managers, such as monitoring performance and producing reports from large amounts of data. It could even be argued that technology is better, or at least more consistent, at these tasks than human beings. But there is another point that is more important here: that the nature of many modern jobs is more akin to the role of the old craftsmen and women.

Increasingly, modern jobs are based on knowledge as technology replaces vast swathes of manual labour. These employees are essentially experts in their specific roles, but this also means that they are likely to be able to self-organise in small teams without the need for a manager directing the project. In some ways we have returned to working practices of the past, where skilled craftsmen and women worked together on large projects. These modern-day experts in their fields know *what needs to be done and how*, and managers are increasingly viewed with irritation as they try to impose their own ideas on a project without having the necessary expert understanding. Many companies nowadays have self-managing teams and have shifted the manager's role to that of mentor.

Although the future may seem uncertain for many managers, a slight shift in perspective can reveal some positives. For one, as the need for managers reduces, those who are left will have to help guide companies through the transition, and therefore their skills will be highly valued. In addition, managers will have to develop new skills that they could possibly use in coaching self-managed teams through complex aspects of projects. Some of these skills could include understanding the psychological dynamics of teams, communication techniques, stress management and improving innovation.

However, as the new look of management develops, it will become just another part of the changing landscape of the workplace. The previous division of labour between workers and managers essentially paved the way for the idea of career progression or advancement, which has since dominated our attitude towards employment. Younger workers currently see advancement at work very differently, but this is not to say that they are any less ambitious than preceding generations. They are looking for opportunities to develop personal skills or increase their knowledge, and this clearly highlights the difference between the old and new practices. Previously, career progression was outward facing, through the monitoring and controlling of others, while nowadays people are more inward looking with a focus on personal fulfilment and increasing their effectiveness. All this is part of the reimagining of work, a process accelerated by today's technological revolution where the buzzwords are 'remote working', 'work-life balance' and 'personal growth' instead of climbing the ladder to management.

31 In paragraph 1, according to the writer, how have employees' career objectives have changed recently?

A People prefer working in teams without strict hierarchies.

B They have set their sights higher than previous generations.

C Fewer are motivated by the idea of taking on responsibility.

D Management has become a more attractive progression route.

32 Paragraph 2 says that the challenge for early managers was:

A staff discipline.

B commanding respect.

C quality control.

D training workers.

33 In paragraph 3, what does the writer think is ironic?

A People's newfound positive attitude to technology.

B The desire to introduce old crafting techniques.

C That technology can so easily replace managers.

D How changes in the workplace are coming full circle.

34 Paragraph 4 says that the traditional role of manager is disappearing because:

A their expertise goes out of date quickly.

B their knowledge is often disputed.

C they serve no obvious purpose.

D they tend not to be good team players.

35 In paragraph 5, how does the writer see the future of management?

A In an overwhelmingly positive light.

B As a career to be avoided at all costs.

C Yet to be defined with any clarity.

D Not likely to stand the test of time.

36 The writer concludes that:

A companies now need to provide their employees with a wider range of benefits.

B the relationship between individuals and their work has evolved.

C employee satisfaction is achieved through a sense of belonging rather than loyalty.

D employers and employees both value interpersonal skills highly nowadays.

You are going to read an extract from a book. Seven paragraphs have been removed. Select from the paragraphs (A–H) the one that fits each gap (37–43). There is one extra paragraph that you do not need to use.

The Empty Shells of Antarctica

Generally, the coldest, driest and windiest continent, Antarctica is a trial for the human body to withstand, so I was naturally apprehensive about my expedition to Mawson's Huts, a remote outpost in that frozen continent. Undertaking one of the most epic journeys I'd ever be likely to take, I dressed in layers of thermal and waterproof clothing in order to shield my rather pampered body from the sub-zero conditions that awaited me.

37	

When I arrived at the huts, the temperature was –7 degrees Celsius – which we could consider to be summertime there, I was told – and it felt bitterly cold with a wind that whipped into the very heart of me. How men could survive there all these years ago doesn't bear thinking about, yet, upon entering the hut, echoes of their lives, and their successes, still resounded in such small details as their names on their bunks, and names of familiar places they could think about while there.

38	

Since the 1970s, continual efforts have been made to preserve the structure, as it is just one of six surviving sites from what is known as the Heroic Era of Antarctic Explorations, a time in the early 19th century when the first explorers arrived there. It was perhaps given the name 'heroic' as the conditions were perilous, and the expeditions' aims were mainly to further our understanding of the environment.

39	

This may seem incredible, seeing as Antarctica has no permanent human population. There are on average 3,000 people stationed there during the year and this number drops to around 1,000 in the more challenging winter months. This means that buildings greatly outnumber the population and, on top of this, most people are concentrated in a few active research stations. The fact that this beautiful wilderness is littered with disused buildings is something that is extremely problematic and the focus of international action.

40	

Naturally, things are changing. There is a more general awareness in the world that humans need to limit their impact, and such policies as the Madrid Protocol, which includes, alongside wide-ranging rules on commercial activity in the Antarctic, regulations citing that any abandoned structures should be carefully removed. However, there are still many tourist trips made to the continent, including to Mawson's Huts, and there are still thousands of empty outposts to see there.

41	

The 1959 Antarctic Treaty declared that only countries conducting substantial research activity in Antarctica could have a vote in decisions about the continent's future. This, naturally, saw heightened interest in the area and construction, but for political purposes rather than true research goals.

42	

The footprint of the Mawson expedition would have been relatively minor in comparison to what we see today. The high-tech bases typically serve to conduct a range of activities that contaminate the local environment, from noise and visual pollution to discharge of sewage and energy use. Of course, these elements are necessary for scientists to have a comfortable existence on the island, but they are certainly at odds with preservation of the natural environment.

43	

A The land and the wildlife that live on it are extremely sensitive due to the fact that they have remained in an environment virtually untouched by unknown invasive species for thousands of years. This fragility, coupled with the careless introduction of human activity, can leave indelible effects on the landscape. Such effects include the unintentional introduction of invasive species, and the irresponsible disposal of waste for human-related activities.

B There is no easy resolution to this dilemma. Some academics have called for research stations to be shared between countries to limit the human footprint on the continent, but continued smooth participation in such projects between countries isn't an easy endeavour. Another solution could be the introduction of further regulations, but this hasn't seemed to work in the past. Maybe the answer lies in the gradual change of our collective mindset in respect of our natural world. As more and more people realise that we as humans have a responsibility to protect rather than transform the environment, maybe governments will start listening.

C One reason for this is that these obligations do not apply to buildings that were constructed over a certain number of years ago. This is largely because these sites have historical significance, and there may be environmental repercussions from their removal after so much time. Yet it was another policy decision that perhaps caused the initial boom of these buildings.

D It's essentially a wonderful social history that is literally frozen in time. I could see a candle in a tin and a book, *The Methods of Mr Ames*, which conjured up images of someone in their sleeping bag reading by candlelight. However, despite these wonderful historical details, nature is constantly trying the reclaim this settlement, as can be seen by the ice crystals creeping into the building.

E The hostile nature of the environment there may have limited human presence, but sadly not sufficiently to prevent changes to the natural ecoculture on the continent. Despite what we may think, Antarctica has an abundance of flora and fauna, many of which have been affected by the growing appearance of man and his structures on their land. Yet, many claim this is a problem that cannot and should not be reversed.

F However, and although this is one of a smattering of structures of historic significance on the continent, it is far from unusual as abandoned buildings in Antarctica go. In fact, there are around 5,000 structures on the continent, many of which are deserted, and the buildings there range from research stations to churches and lighthouses.

G Sir Douglas Mawson and his team didn't have such luxuries when they constructed these small structures over a century ago. With his group of explorers and scientists, they established the base in order to provide ground-breaking information about the environment and wildlife on the continent, even sending the first radio communications from the continent back to Australia, documenting their undertaking.

H Nowadays, the continent is peppered with run-down structures from the 20th century to the modern state-of-the-art bases that are currently being used by researchers. We can only imagine what Sir Douglas Mawson would have thought about these kinds of developments and the use of the land.

You are going to read an article about people's opinions of festivals. For questions 44–53, choose from the people (A–D) using the separate answer sheet. The people may be chosen more than once.

Which person:

describes a festival that prioritised the involvement of local businesses from the outset?	**44**	
thinks that festival organisers are indifferent to certain festival-goers?	**45**	
provides an explanation for why some people dislike the effects of festivals	**46**	
confesses that staging a festival involves a real commitment?	**47**	
explains a downside to having a wide range of performers at festivals?	**48**	
describes an imbalance in the provision of facilities?	**49**	
mentions their preference for a more formal approach to festivals?	**50**	
talks about being dissatisfied with the narrow target audience of many festivals?	**51**	
acknowledges the financial benefits of festivals?	**52**	
says that they are fussy about the types of festival they feel comfortable attending?	**53**	

Evaluating Different Festivals – A Personal Perspective

People share what they love about festivals, as well as their pet hates

A Hanifa

I suffer from mobility difficulties, and so need a wheelchair to get around. This makes festivals a nightmare since the majority of them fail to provide adequate access for people in my situation. This is especially true when compared to other music and performance venues, such as concert halls and theatres where disabled access is a legal requirement nowadays. The employees in these venues have received training in health and safety for disabled people and are always available to help. I could probably manage to navigate one of those places without any such assistance, but festivals are the exact opposite. I know some people think that this is just disappointing, but, as far as I'm concerned, it's discrimination as it feels like the organisers are either ignoring us or can't be bothered to find solutions to our access problems. I don't imagine that improving disabled access to festivals would be an insurmountable problem, but organisers just don't seem to be willing to devote the necessary time and effort. At least nowadays a significant number of festivals offer some form of online access, but I would really appreciate it if more an effort were made for wheelchair users overall.

B Min

When I think of festivals, music is the last thing that comes to mind and I suppose that's because festivals in the region I live in are predominantly focused on gastronomy. It's very agricultural here, and that, coupled with the inaccessible coastal location, has created many food festivals, some of which attract lots of tourists looking for things off the beaten track. Food tourism brings visitors from far and wide, and although it's boosted our local economy considerably over the last couple of decades, it's not without its disadvantages – most of which centre around the issue of vehicle access. Getting to some of the small villages where these festivals are located is extremely challenging for buses and caravans, and locals are none too pleased with the disruption all this causes to their everyday lives. However, all that is usually forgotten as soon as the event is in full swing because people are having such a fantastic time. As far as I'm concerned, these events are far better than sitting in a field with a picnic listening to music because there are tables and chairs, and proper plates and glasses, as well as opportunities to meet people from different cultures as you sample the amazing produce on offer.

C Yoshie

The roaring crowds and lack of space at music festivals are overwhelming for me to say the least, not to mention the huge capacity of many festivals nowadays that makes them disorientating, unpleasant experiences. However, that's not to say that I never attend any. I'm just selective and ensure that I research an event thoroughly beforehand to evaluate its suitability. Those that are more appealing tend to be literary festivals as they often require considerable concentration on the part of the audience, which forces everyone to listen attentively and quietly. Recently I attended an online festival and was delighted not to have to miss any performances as all sessions were recorded and subsequently made available to ticket holders afterwards, a decision by the organisers that definitely enhanced my overall experience of the event. That's something that gets on my nerves at live festivals because I always end up having to miss something I want to see as a result of performance clashes. Although I understand that predicting festival goers' favourites is an impossible task, I get frustrated by not having access to the programme in advance, and sometimes I feel a little short changed, like I haven't had real value for money because I've had to miss some performances or talk that I was really keen on seeing.

D Iker

I'm on the committee for the summer festival held in our town each August. The festival came about from a group of parents complaining about a lack of provision for families with children, especially those from poorer backgrounds or those with disabilities. We wanted to centre the festival around the concepts of inclusivity and diversity in our community, so we gave priority to performers and caterers who were local residents themselves. Anyway, within hours of putting up a website and posters asking for participants, we were inundated with applicants for food stalls and the music stage, as well as countless children's entertainers. It was quite remarkable, and we were delighted, but of course that was when we realised just how much work the organisation would entail. We were slightly daunted by the prospect to be honest, but we needn't have worried as the first festival was a real success story and we even had a journalist from the local newspaper come to cover the event, which enabled us to get some funding from the local council for the following year. Since then, it's gone from strength to strength and has created a real sense of community for all those involved.

Name ______________________ Date ____________

Part 5

Mark the appropriate answer.

0	A	B	C ▬	D
31	A	B	C	D
32	A	B	C	D
33	A	B	C	D
34	A	B	C	D
35	A	B	C	D
36	A	B	C	D

Part 6

Add the appropriate answer.

37		38		39		40		41		42		43	

Part 7

Add the appropriate answer.

44		45	
46		47	
48		49	
50		51	
52		53	

Cambridge C2 Proficiency Reading: Parts 5–7

Test 6

You are going to read an extract from a novel. For questions 31–36, mark the appropriate answer (A, B, C or D) that you think fits best according to the text.

The Comics

Cleaning is profoundly tiresome for me at the best of times, and contemplating having to return to my family home and whip my parents' attic into shape so that they could have it converted it into a studio did not fill me with any enthusiasm whatsoever. In their eighties, they couldn't realistically undertake a task like that without some assistance with the bulk of it, and besides, I desperately needed a bit of respite away from the city. I was behind on my rent and my music career appeared to be at an effective standstill. Spending my time playing half-empty bars and restaurants for barely minimum wage wasn't the dream I'd yearned for, and most nights I felt like I received about as much recognition as the furniture did.

So, I loaded up my truck and travelled back to my parents' place for the winter. Although it might feel a bit unsettling to be back in the family home, I knew my assistance would be invaluable for the odd jobs that had been neglected recently, not to mention the quality time we'd be able to share, and, after all they'd sacrificed for me, putting in a few hours of labour was the least I could do. It was being back amongst all the memories with time on my hands that prompted me to start reassessing my life. The future, instead of looking like an amazing blank canvas, felt like a bleak and empty space, and with every path my imagination took, the avenues appeared to be closed. I was coming to the slow and reluctant realisation that I might have to make this stay permanent, which was a far cry from the future I'd dreamed of as a hopeful child for my forty-five-year-old self.

But little did I know that the tide was about to turn. While I was sifting through all the junk in the attic, I came across a box of old superhero comics that had been my dad's childhood obsession. It was obvious that these were his pride and joy, with every cherished edition in mint condition and individually wrapped. Dad was delighted to be reacquainted with his boyhood and we spent the afternoon browsing through the pages while he reminisced over the good old days. It even triggered my own recollections! I asked him if he wanted to keep them, but he declined insisting that they'd be better off being passed on to someone who'd get the same kick out of them that he once had. He told me that the second-hand shop in town might be able to do something with them. So, I packed them into the trunk of my truck for the night, with the intention to see whether the second-hand shop might sell them on along with the other junk I'd discovered.

In town the following day, I went in the only store that would be interested in the old clutter from my parents' attic, the second-hand store called McBride's that traded in all manner of things. On entering, intending to drop everything off and make a dash, I casually mentioned to the owner what I'd been up to the afternoon before and how we'd pored over dad's old comics. She looked at me knowingly and suggested that they might be of sizeable value depending on when they had been published. So, we hauled all the comics out onto the counter and began searching online for information on each edition, to see if we could strike it lucky with any of them. We couldn't believe our eyes when we typed in 'All Star Comics Issue 8', and the search results revealed that, it being the first edition to feature Wonder Woman, a copy had recently sold at auction for over $900,000, and here it was, another first-edition copy with no tears and no blemishes, and in my now rather sweaty shaking hands!

With our windfall, my parents were able to construct their dream studio, as well as go on the world cruise they'd always dreamed of, and they furnished me with the money for an altogether different studio in which we could achieve our shared ambitions. I recorded my first album with my newly formed and named backing group, "The All-Stars", and that's what propelled me to have my very first country hit. And now, even with six albums under my belt, I rarely forget that life's opportunities are few and far between, and that my entire future was transformed by my parent's generosity, a shopkeeper's honesty and one long-forgotten old comic!

31 How did the writer feel about his work?

A He didn't get paid as much as he'd hoped.

B He felt that his talent was being wasted.

C He felt that he wasn't appreciated.

D He thought the venues were below him.

32 Why did the writer go back to his parents?

A To take a break from city life.

B To help them with a task.

C To spend time with them.

D To look after them.

33 In paragraph two, how does the writer feel about his life?

A It hadn't turned out as he'd expected.

B He feels bitter about his choices.

C He regrets his past optimism.

D He thinks he's destined to be unlucky.

34 He and his dad spent the afternoon:

A talking about the comics they had found in the attic.

B describing how the world has changed since they were young.

C looking back at their childhoods with fondness.

D sorting through all the issues of the comics.

35 What is the writer's initial attitude to the comics?

A They are particularly memorable.

B They can give others happiness.

C They shouldn't be thrown out.

D They're nothing out of the ordinary.

36 What sums up the main idea expressed in the text?

A It's never too late to try again.

B Things can turn around.

C Finding happiness in the details.

D Making a fresh start.

You are going to read an extract from an article. Seven paragraphs have been removed. Select from the paragraphs (A–H) the one that fits each gap (37–43). There is one extra paragraph that you do not need to use.

Women in the Sciences

The expression 'behind every great man is a great woman' has been in use since the mid-1940s, but undoubtedly the meaning behind this saying has been true for centuries. This phrase more literally refers to both the practical and emotional support women can give to their significant others who toil for success, yet it also infers the disheartening idea that perhaps women haven't previously had the opportunity to revel in their own successes.

37 ______

Rosalind Franklin is a name you might recognise now, but just seventy years ago her research was overlooked in terms of its instrumental contribution to the discovery of the structure of DNA. The acclaim for the discovery, however, and even the Nobel Prize, went to three men, Francis Crick, James Watson and Maurice Wilkins, without any reference to Franklin's input.

38 ______

Incidents like this have occurred so often within the field that the term 'the Matilda Effect' was coined in 1993 by Margaret W. Rossiter, a scientist who has devoted her career to shining a light on the generally overlooked female scientists who were rather brazenly excluded from the history books. One of Rossiter's aims has been that a renewed focus on successes of female scientists in history may encourage more women to enter the field of science.

39 ______

Still, efforts continue to publicise the overlooked female scientists in history. From a series of pop art posters showcasing pioneering scientists like Ada Lovelace and Chien-Shiung Wu, to even rectifying past injustices by amending search-engine results to reflect real contributions, the cause of female scientists is gradually strengthening.

40 ______

However, perhaps scientific traditions need to be rectified not just by the gender divide but by using a broader lens. There is plenty of discussion nowadays about how women have frequently been underestimated and overlooked by their male colleagues, as illustrated by the examples above. However, rather than this being a pure case of gender inequality, perhaps the defining factor is simply the historically unequal power relationship between parties.

41 ______

While we see efforts to shine a light on the females whose contributions have been unnoticed by the general scientific community, maybe it will be a little harder to find those men who were overlooked in favour of someone with a greater stature. After all, it is near impossible to explore these kinds of power relationships so long after the event.

42 ______

Perhaps science will never reach an ideal world of an individual's contribution being equal to their reward, but opening this subject up for reflection and discussion is essential, and equal input for equal credit is just one aim to strive for. It has encouraged females into the sciences already, and both the terms 'the Matilda Effect' and 'the Matthew Effect' by their very use are making inroads into highlighting inequalities.

43 ______

A The Matthew Effect can be summarised as the way in which disproportionate recognition is attributed to someone who is more famous or in a position of power. So, for example, an acclaimed scientist will naturally get more credit than a lesser-known researcher, even if their work is comparable. This may seem a given, as the most powerful or famous team member often leads the research, but that doesn't mean there isn't a talent in the background contributing the lion's share of the scientific endeavour.

B Due to this growing number of complaints, especially those from female research scientists at universities, some institutions are now addressing the issue. They are doing this in a twofold manner: by shining a light on incidences in their own institutions that have been caused by a gender power inequality and offering further opportunities and support to women in the sciences. This has been heartily welcomed by the wider scientific community.

C One effort we can all make is to encourage a shift in people's attitudes in general and ensure that this shift is also reflected in the world of science. We can see flaws in the past and the present, as illustrated, and research shows that male and female stereotypes still exist when it comes to the perceived quality of female work, and common sense can tell us that the most powerful names get the most credit. However, that doesn't mean things should remain the same in the years to come.

D However, perhaps the views on female scientists are too deeply embedded in the scientific community for the situation to be rectified overnight. A 2013 paper found that male scientists and more masculine topics, regardless of who wrote them, are perceived as being of higher scientific quality. In the investigation, graduate students of both sexes rated abstracts of papers that were assigned a fake male or female name, and the fake male names were more highly rated overall. In addition, the same study indicated that men are more desirable as collaboration partners.

E Never has this bleak interpretation been more accurate than in the field of science, where women have usually taken a back seat, and not by choice. Examples of this can be observed throughout history, as far back as the 12th century, when physician Trotula of Salerno had her ground-breaking work attributed to men, and in the modern day where female science professionals still sometimes struggle for appropriate recognition.

F For instance, try finding out about 'the Dean Method' online. A quick google will offer you little mention of that particular term, but instead it will return a multitude of results for scientist Alice Augusta Ball. The Dean Method, published by chemist and academic Arthur L. Dean, was widely known as the cure for leprosy, an infectious condition that used to cause severe skin sores and often resulted in limbs withering. However, it eventually transpired that, upon the death of Alice Augusta Ball in 1916, Arthur Dean had taken her efforts and claimed them as his own.

G You may be reading this article thinking that this is an issue you are powerless to change, but you make up part of the world we share, and a sea change only happens through the individual shifts in people's opinions. So, the next time you read about the latest greatest discovery or the history of science, it might well be worth remembering that behind every big name, there are many others who make valuable, if not *the most* valuable contributions to research.

H Even in one of the winner's memoirs, we can see the attitude displayed towards her, with the mentioned colleague even failing to call her by her proper name, preferring nicknames that served to belittle her role in this ground-breaking finding. The author did acknowledge her achievements in his book, but this admission was fifteen years too late.

You are going to read an extract from a newspaper article about modern cities. For questions 44–53, select the person (A–E) using the separate answer sheet. The person may be selected more than once.

In which sections are the following mentioned?

Cities need to focus on how they can reduce one-time consumption.	**44**	
A fix that will take a varying amount of effort.	**45**	
Cities have a common reputation that overlooks their positive aspects.	**46**	
An acknowledgement that the solution may be disagreeable to some.	**47**	
Our cities are designed in a way that makes us feel detached from others.	**48**	
How people can become more integrated in cities.	**49**	
Some people are ignoring problems that we should be tackling.	**50**	
Cities have been left to grow virtually unchecked.	**51**	
Future enhancements will be determined by fundamental elements of construction.	**52**	
The reputation of cities and the reality of cities are different.	**53**	

The Modern City

Jacob Moore spoke with five city dwellers to find out what they think are the problems with modern cities.

A Iain Bracewell

It goes without saying that modern cities are somewhat problematic, simply because we don't have the capacity for all the people who already live here, let alone the millions who see cities as a potential destination. Therefore, in my mind, it's vital that we become a bit more imaginative about how we utilise city space. We're going to be somewhat reliant on technology to help us with this, by, for example, developing materials that we can use to build higher, slimmer and underground. This might seem less than ideal for the average city dweller, especially the notion having to spend a proportion of time below ground, but it might be the only practical solution to what the data suggest if we want to avoid cities growing at an uncontrolled rate across our countryside. And time is of the essence; we can't put this kind of research and development off it while the population growth remains uncontained.

B Raphael Arco

Cities are often seen in a bad light, but I think this is undeserved because they offer so much to so many. The fact is that cities are synonymous with opportunity, for employment, culture, you name it! That's not to say they are utopias without any room for improvement, but I think we can solve a great majority of the issues affecting cities by addressing their infrastructure. People often cite their bugbears as being issues of convenience such as streets that aren't walkable or road networks that are too dense, or even lack of space for increased public transport. Devote serious attention on improving these elements and cities will become far more liveable places with, in turn, generally all-round happier residents! This might consist of tweaks or alternatively, in certain contexts, starting from scratch to fundamentally redesign systems, but the benefits outweigh the sacrifices as they'd offer valuable solutions to how modern city life affects the natural environment and how well people gel together as a community.

C Jenna Crawford

We need to face up to the fact that most cities aren't the glorious places that they are painted to be, and that, for the majority of the inhabitants, the streets aren't paved with gold. There is a big difference between the haves and have-nots, and while city life is a consumer paradise for the former, members of the latter category are completely locked out of the benefits cities bring and often lack fundamental services such as clean water or sanitation. Why this is still allowed in the modern world I'll never know, yet the powers that be seem disinclined to do anything but sweep the issue under the carpet.. Property rental prices are also excessive, and this just gets to the point where you've got huge families living cramped in just two rooms, or people receiving full-time salaries with little to no chance of getting on the housing ladder. I understand that people think there are valuable opportunities to be had in cities, but, let's face it, there are still plenty of people for whom opportunity has passed by.

D Caroline Birkenstein

Our cities right now are in dire straits. We've got an affordable housing and ecological crisis in nearly every city on Earth, and it's crucial that we concentrate our efforts on these matters if we want our cities to continue to thrive. We can accomplish this by creating and promoting more sharing and communal practices, like coworking spaces or apartment buildings with common spaces for eating, socialising and exercising, and these, of course, shouldn't be extravagantly priced. It might not seem obvious, but it's initiatives like these that help people form communities, and this community atmosphere encourages people to care more about their surroundings. Cities are also a massive drain on resources, and we need to identify strategies to counter this and close the loop when it comes to this. With this in mind, we should ask ourselves how one excess can be used to give power to something else. This kind of sustainability could be the key to making our cities much healthier places for individuals, the community and the surroundings we live in.

E Doug de Souza

Cities today have one major problem that we need to curb, and that is urban sprawl. At the moment, cities are like these huge sprawls, just spreading and spreading, and the further out you go, the bigger plot each homeowner has and the more spacious all the services are. This really has a negative effect on so many elements of our lives. Firstly, it makes us more isolated; we're behind fences, and this is where feelings of difference and fear can stem from. We need integration to help people consider themselves a part of something, but, furthermore, sprawl increases the urban footprint significantly, and people start becoming dependent on their cars, simply because it's not convenient to go anywhere on foot – rather, driving becomes the preferred option. I mean, I don't think it takes a scientist to see the environmental problems that can arise from that.

Name ______________________________ **Date** ______________

Part 5

Mark the appropriate answer.

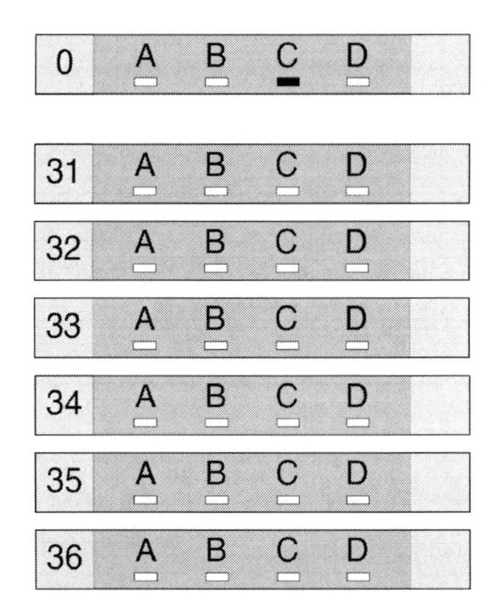

Part 6

Add the appropriate answer.

37	38	39	40	41	42	43

Part 7

Add the appropriate answer.

44	45
46	47
48	49
50	51
52	53

Cambridge C2 Proficiency
Reading: Parts 5–7

Test 7

You are going to read an extract from a book. For questions 31–36, mark the appropriate answer (A, B, C or D) that you think fits best according to the text.

Addressing the Problem of Water Scarcity

Despite 70% of the world's surface being covered with water, less than 3% of that is actually drinkable and, based on factors ranging from agricultural practices to climate change and daily habits, water scarcity is fast becoming a serious problem in many countries around the globe. The problem of scarcity – in other words, having insufficient water – is categorised as being physical (happening in places where supply cannot meet demand) or economic (occurring in areas that have plenty of water but don't have good management systems). Broadly speaking, the causes of water scarcity are related to the rapid rise of the global population and the associated issues that this has brought, and the predictions in many parts of the world are that the population will continue to rise for several decades. This suggests that rather than lamenting the journey to this point, we would be better off focusing on solutions, especially given that the causes have been written about extensively and are very well understood, which is not the case for the solutions.

Solutions for water scarcity should primarily be context-specific if they are to work, and must include experts, organisations and charities that can provide insight into the particular challenges. For example, there is no point in poorer nations engaging expert engineers from overseas to help with the infrastructure for water management systems if the resulting system is not affordable or able to withstand the climatic conditions of the region. Too often collaborations on projects like this turn into vanity projects for the foreign companies in much the same way as high-end commercial projects, such as the building of a luxury hotel or impressive bridge. Workable solutions will need to understand the influences of geology, the environment and the influences of local culture to be successful and will likely be a combination of technology and a change in human behaviour. One immediate approach is to provide incentives for people to upgrade more old-fashioned machines to water-efficient ones, such as toilets and showers that use considerably less water. Another is to adjust the cost based on consumption by installing water meters in homes, something that has not been widely reported in the press. It appears that there is little incentive for governments to encourage uptake among households as any change would negatively affect voters on low incomes and families.

A better alternative to punishing such bad consumer behaviour is for governments to invest in educating their populations. For example, many are unaware of the amount of water used to produce the food we consume. The meat industry is a case in point in which vast quantities of water are required, yet the general public is largely ignorant of this. Education on water conservation methods should come from a commitment to ensuring people have the relevant scientific evidence presented to them, otherwise they will be unable to make informed decisions. There is already enough fake science floating around on the internet and it is important not to add to it.

An additional approach that is well worth thinking about is tackling the problem through multiple small lifestyles changes rather than national or international projects. After all, the situation affects millions of people, so anything that ordinary people can do without disrupting their lives too much would be a bonus. Research from behavioural science has shown that when people have to opt into a system, the likelihood of their doing so is reduced because of the increased effort involved. Rainwater collection for uses such as cleaning and washing clothes is an example of a small change. It is both low-cost and easily implementable since local councils could supply households with containers, allowing them to begin water conservation immediately.

We must also remember that better management of the environment plays a large part in maintaining the water supplies on the planet. There are certain ecosystems, such as forests, marshes and wetlands, that naturally process, collect and filter water, and preserving these natural systems is essential. Unfortunately, the practices of many commercial industries are at odds with conservation strategies for these ecosystems and so continue to be widespread. Making laws to protect these natural systems is another cost-effective way to change both attitudes and behaviour to water, and it's high time that governments stepped up and took control of the situation if we are to succeed in protecting our most precious resource.

31 In the first paragraph, the writer argues that:

A forecasting the locations of water shortages is a pointless activity.

B people have approached the shortage of water from the wrong angle.

C the causes of water shortages are too complex to understand.

D few of the proposed solutions to water shortages are viable.

32 In paragraph 2, what does the writer say about infrastructure collaborations?

A Local skills are valued.

B Costs are excessive.

C Planning is fundamental.

D Resources are inadequate.

33 Why are water meters not widely promoted?

A They are potentially politically damaging.

B Installation costs are beyond the reach of the poor.

C The media are more interested in other solutions.

D Their efficiency has been questioned.

34 In paragraph 3, the writer suggests that people should be taught about water scarcity by:

A providing a public information service online.

B publicising the impact of the meat industry.

C targeting government information campaigns.

D improving public access to appropriate research.

35 In paragraph 4, the writer advocates simple solutions because:

A they are more effective for the environment.

B successful results can be obtained more quickly.

C governments prefer straightforward processes.

D psychological studies have shown that uptake is higher.

36 In the final paragraph, what point is the writer making about tackling water scarcity?

A Controlling harmful commercial practices is essential.

B Human beings should not interfere with natural processes.

C Countries with strict laws are making more progress.

D Some conservation measures are ill-advised.

You are going to read an extract from a short story. Seven paragraphs have been removed. Select from the paragraphs (A–H) the one that fits each gap (37–43). There is one extra paragraph that you do not need to use.

Sleepwalker

The first thing I remembered was the blare of a horn and stiff wind brushing past me, causing me to spin and collapse to the ground. As my head made contact with the ground, I could feel cold concrete beneath my cheek and I became dizzily aware of cold night air that stung my nose as I breathed. This felt all too realistic to my senses, and my brain started whirring into gear.

37	

The carriageway wasn't extremely busy, it being the dead of night, but I still knew I was in terrible danger. The lights of a truck, growing threateningly in the distance, told me all I needed to know. I clambered to my knees and feet, and made a run for it. One lane, two lanes, just in time. Looking down at my bare feet and pyjamas, I must have appeared as a nightmare vision to the sporadic late-night travellers passing this three-lane stretch.

38	

"This is one of the most disturbing cases I've heard in years, and we undoubtedly have to take some drastic measures immediately, starting with preventing you from exiting your house in this kind of state. Tell me everything." If I had been mildly concerned before, I was absolutely horrified now. Here I was, expecting comforting words and perhaps some medication and an opportunity to recharge the batteries, and the reaction I received couldn't have been more different.

39	

He studiously scribbled away, interjecting with the odd nod or question to clarify any vagaries. This was a man who didn't suffer fools gladly, and he could see right through my weak attempts to make light of my problems, and my woeful inaction. Peering over his glasses, he suggested that we take multiple approaches in order to deal with the problem, starting with a visit to a sleep clinic along with keeping a regular diary of episodes and my corresponding frame of mind, and with my wife locking doors and windows so that I could stay away from any harm.

40	

It turned out to be far easier than keeping track of my days, nights and accompanying state of mind. It just took up so much of my day that was already packed with work meetings and deadlines. Juggling so many commitments was becoming a trial, and was making my moods, and condition, worse as far as I was concerned. If my wife hadn't locked us in, I dread to think where I may have ended up.

41	

Apparently, it's far better to address the causes rather than just patch over the symptoms, which often proves inferior and temporary in their relief. It seemed I had really angered him as we sat in silence for the next twenty minutes while he leafed through my diary and I fidgeted in rather a disgruntled and wholly uncomfortable state, contemplating how this whole exercise was turning out to be a complete and utter waste of time.

42	

I couldn't deny that this was true, and it was like a puzzle coming into place right in front of me. There was an answer to this problem, and I had held the key to it all this time. It's truly incredible what your subconscious is capable of, and I've come to realise it's absolutely essential to put your own wellbeing first.

43	

A On the motorway, I considered, apprehensively, what lay before me. From what I'd read it sounded like something from a science fiction film, with sensors placed all over my body, and video equipment recording my every move. However, I was willing to try anything after the dreadful scare I'd had. When I arrived, it was almost identical to my preconceptions, and I was convinced it was the least conducive place in which to drop off, but I had, at the very least, to give it a shot.

B Then, snapping me out of my fixation on a nearby willow and back to the present situation, he delivered his epiphany. He explained that my condition came from what he considered to be one fundamental determiner: stress. He illustrated that each episode had occurred during a period of time in which I felt my workload had gotten on top of me.

C It was then that it dawned on me that this couldn't be some hyper-realistic dream, but instead it was real life, and I was in genuine danger. I longed desperately for my eyes to remain shut and hoped that I'd suddenly come to in my bed, softly nestled under my duvet, but I knew that I had I had no option but to face up to what I suspected, and, as I lifted my lids, the extent of my situation was far beyond anything I could have imagined.

D I don't think anyone could forget the shock and fear of awakening on a major carriageway, and it sometimes still haunts me, but thankfully only in my imagination now as I've learned to make essential changes to my lifestyle. In real life, I hope only to see roads from behind the wheel of my car.

E I was in quite a bad temper on my return visit, and I took it out on the doctor a little, rather sternly protesting that I could see little improvements from such laborious tasks, and that I would much prefer some kind of medication rather than this holistic (or what I considered rather bogus) approach. Well, I got quite a stern response in return.

F This is what prompted my visits with Dr Potter. After all, I couldn't let this lie, or I'd be in danger of seriously harming either myself and/or the others around me. Sleepwalking is a common-enough problem and, having come to on the garden lawn or the living room, I used to take it with a pinch of salt, but try thinking that when you come around in the lane of a highway.

G I couldn't believe my ears when the doctor told me. After all this time the answer was right under my nose, but how could he have solved this just from listening to the accounts from me and my wife? He obviously had far more skill that I had given him credit for.

H Pinpointing where it started was more difficult than I imagined, and, as I tried to wrack my brains over the details, I realised I had been turning a blind eye to this problem for far too long. What I did recognise, though, was how each episode had gradually worsened over time, and I began to feel rather embarrassed that I had shunned my wife's appeals that I sought help. As happens all too often, when you begin to lay out a history, it becomes all the more clear to the narrator.

You are going to read an extract from an article on interior design. For questions 44–53, select the expert (A–E) using the separate answer sheet. The expert may be selected more than once.

Which person:

suggests that interior designers could upskill themselves to meet customer expectations?	**44**	
is not convinced that it is worth speculating on the future of interior design?	**45**	
supports the movement of interior design towards a wider customer base?	**46**	
thinks that there is a connection between interior design and social mobility?	**47**	
is disappointed that interior design has become bland for everyone involved?	**48**	
believes technology will completely transform the industry?	**49**	
suggests that interior design will become more environmentally friendly?	**50**	
believes that the future of interior design will be comparable to changes in another industry?	**51**	
predicts that designers will work alongside other professionals to create the interiors of the future?	**52**	
says that there is little evidence that technology will replace interior designers?	**53**	

The Future of Interior Design

Five designers talk about the changes they see on the horizon

A Antonio Maroles

I'm optimistic about the future, actually, because no industry gets the luxury of staying the same forever; otherwise innovation never happens. For me, much of what is changing is exciting, especially how technology will open up the sector to more people. Interior design used to only be accessible by a select few, whereas now it's much more egalitarian and affordable, and this will bring opportunities for designers everywhere. Apps that allow customers to visualise designs and 'walk through' 3D rooms are going to revolutionise how we do things, and customers will also be able to recruit designers from anywhere in the world. All this would have been unthinkable a decade ago when all these image apps didn't exist, but they've really opened up the possibilities to interact with clients and increase that level of personalised service. And this gives designers far more scope to develop their own personal style, too. Years ago, everyone tended to follow the same trends promoted in magazines and by fabric or wallpaper companies, but that approach is dead now that anyone can create their own distinctive style, whichever walk of life they come from, and I'm fully behind it.

B Jeannette Harrison

So many interior designers are panicking that technology is going to put them out of a job in the next few years, but I find all this gloomy talk quite depressing and quite unlikely in the foreseeable future. The latest market analysis is not telling us that people want their homes to go high-tech anytime soon. In fact. quite the opposite seems to be true if you look carefully at the research. There are real concerns around privacy connected to smart technology in our homes, so in my view the fear of technology is leading the profession up a blind alley. What people are looking for, however, is individuality, both at the high end of the market and the new middle-class customers who can afford to design their homes more to their own tastes due to a wider range of prices. I am slightly concerned about the impact on less technologically minded designers because, although it's not going to take over our jobs, clients will start to expect a basic level of proficiency with design apps.

C Bobbi Zarkowksi

As far as I'm concerned, there's no point in trying to predict the outcomes of this period of change with any certainty. There are all sorts of people saying that the end is in sight for interior designers because consumers can do everything themselves online, but this is an oversimplification of the situation. There are considerable similarities to what went on in the travel sector, so we would do well to analyse the impact of the internet to analyse the impact of the internet for them before wringing our hands in despair. Of course, the internet democratised travel for the masses, but parts of that meant that the type of customer changed significantly. Likewise, interior design has always been seen as a luxury for the wealthy, but not anymore. Whatever the effects over the coming decade there will be winners and losers, and those who survive will harness the internet to their advantage instead of railing against it.

D Martina Davis

I'm really hoping that the future heralds a return to creativity after this horrible period, which I affectionately call the beige stage. I understand that it's important for more people to have access to interior design because increased access reflects a society that has improved living conditions for its citizens. But these people should also be given choice and creativity too, and, unfortunately, what I see around me nowadays is somewhat of a paradox; people have a desire to express their individuality at home in the same way they do through fashion, but this self-expression is often identical. The retail landscape is entirely uninspiring, and I hope the next few years will see a return to innovation and creativity in both customers and designers. I am worried that this will be at odds with sustainability, though, which I wholeheartedly believe must be at the heart of what interior design represents going forward. Cheap furniture from unsustainable wood sources is not the solution, so we've got to try to merge creativity, sustainability and affordability, which is going to be quite a challenge.

E Francesca Cheng

My approach towards design has always drawn on traditional imagery that encapsulates the idea of nature and then applying this inside the home, and this to me is where the future lies because consumers are much more concerned with sustainability now. Based on this I can see interior design having a period of re-evaluation that will likely result in rejecting certain materials or production practices and focusing on innovative ways to be sustainable and stylish together. I predict a lot more design that tries to enhance wellbeing, such as using plants for internal walls or LED lights that use a fraction of the electricity used by other light bulbs. I also think that there'll have to be a lot more collaboration between interior designers and engineers in order to turn these ideas into actual objects or materials that function well at the same time as looking attractive.

Name ______________________ **Date** ____________

Part 5

Mark the appropriate answer.

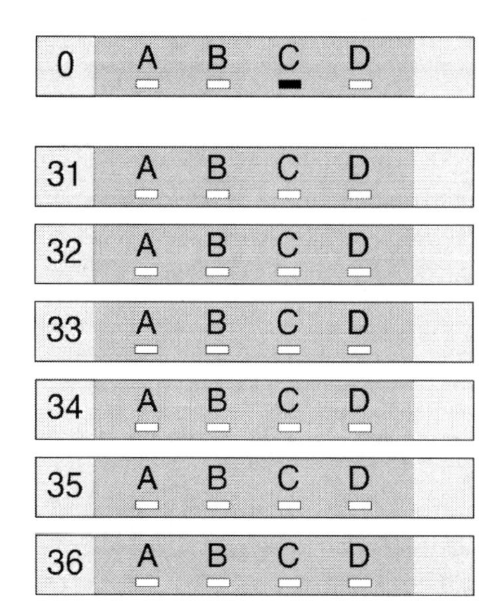

Part 6

Add the appropriate answer.

37	38	39	40	41	42	43

Part 7

Add the appropriate answer.

44	45
46	47
48	49
50	51
52	53

Cambridge C2 Proficiency
Reading: Parts 5–7

Test 8

You are going to read an extract from a novel. For questions 31–36, mark the appropriate answer (A, B, C or D) that you think fits best according to the text.

It's a Long Story!

It was well over thirty years ago now, but Selina can still recall the evening they'd come up with the idea for their business as clearly as a bell. Daniel was cooking and droning on about his miserable workplace and she was gazing absentmindedly out of the window. Academically talented, Daniel had been busy carving out an impressive career in marketing consultancy but had recently become disillusioned by the industry and was looking for something more meaningful. As she half listened, an image popped into her head and suddenly she blurted out, "Well, you could always go back to carving those wooden toys you used to make for your sister's children."

She looked up to find him staring at her, chopping knife in hand, as if he'd been frozen to the spot. It just so happened that besides Daniel's academic talent, he was also a skilled carpenter, which was how their paths had first crossed. Selina had joined the engineering club at university and one evening Daniel walked in on the hunt for a specific tool. Noticing the intricate bicycle carvings poking out of his rucksack, she'd asked to examine them, and then proceeded to ask all sorts of questions about their construction, which delighted him no end. They were really quite impressive for someone self-taught through online videos, but as she would soon learn, that was Daniel all over: a detail-driven obsessive in all things he was passionate about.

The intended recipients of the carvings were Daniel's elder sister's children, whose birthdays were fast approaching, hence the urgency for the woodworking tools. Selina carefully turned them over in her hands inspecting all their moving parts as Daniel explained what he needed. Seconds after he'd finished, she reached into the drawer underneath her desk and pulled out the required tool with a flourish. Later, Daniel would always say that this gesture was what cemented their friendship forever, although she suspected it was artistic license, a way of adding a touch of humour to an otherwise fairly unremarkable story. Anyway, for some unknown reason, that night the memory of those toys had come flooding back and over dinner they wondered aloud whether anyone might consider buying them.

Gradually the idea seduced them more and more until they took the plunge and created a series of miniature hand-carved, wooden toy vehicles. At the outset, their only customers were friends, family and colleagues who, whilst impressed by the quality of the toys, were obviously buying them as a show of support and therefore they couldn't quite work out whether a wider market existed. With hindsight they were able to clearly see the advantages of selling small quantities exclusively to these familiar groups because it allowed for time to develop the product rather than making lots of initial mistakes. Within five years sales had skyrocketed: they were receiving referrals and recommendations and the number of regular customers began to build up.

Despite Daniel's experience working in that flashy marketing agency, word of mouth was how the business grew in the end, but it is surprising how successful that can be when everyone wants what you're selling. Now they had an actual business with offices and employees, and all the associated tedious tasks that those things brought. At some level Selina struggled to see the business as real and, on some mornings, found herself standing at the entrance looking out at their office and marvelling at its sheer existence. To get to this point however, both she and Daniel had been working ten-hour days and had long since abandoned any notion of a social life. If she were completely honest with herself, Selina was wondering how sustainable it all was and whether they needed to have a serious talk about the direction of the business.

The following Tuesday, Selina was working on one of their new toys when Daniel appeared at the doorway and announced in rather a grand manner, "Selina, this is Joanne Hardy, she's an investor and is interested in purchasing part of our business." After we had sat down and exchanged some pleasantries, Joanne turned to Selina and said, "So, how did you two meet?" "Well, ...", Daniel began. At this moment Selina felt a wave of relaxation surge over her, and she turned to Joanne, rolling her eyes. "He loves to tell this story," she said, "but it's pure fabrication!"

31 Selina and Daniel's business idea was born out of:

- **A** frustration with the lack of available career options.
- **B** a desire for a stronger sense of purpose at work.
- **C** the discovery of a hidden creative talent.
- **D** time spent daydreaming about a problem.

32 Daniel and Selina became friends because they:

- **A** believed attention to detail was important.
- **B** shared similar attitudes towards creativity.
- **C** questioned everything that they were taught.
- **D** liked to be emotionally connected to objects.

33 How does Daniel depict their first meeting?

- **A** He says that it was not memorable.
- **B** He omits some of the details.
- **C** He exaggerates it for comic effect.
- **D** He describes it as being hilarious.

34 What aspect of business was difficult when they first started?

- **A** Expanding their range of products.
- **B** Knowing where to advertise.
- **C** Widening their customer base.
- **D** Identifying the scope of the market.

35 How did Selina feel about the development of their business?

- **A** She thought that it was remarkable.
- **B** She viewed the administration as tiresome.
- **C** She worried about its stability.
- **D** She was surprised by its growth rate.

36 How does Selina feel at the end of the story extract?

- **A** Delighted that someone was interested in acquiring their business.
- **B** Concerned that Daniel had made a decision without consulting her.
- **C** Amused that Daniel wanted to explain how they met to a stranger.
- **D** Relieved that Daniel was on the same wavelength as her.

You are going to read an extract from an article. Seven paragraphs have been removed. Select from the paragraphs (A–H) the one that fits each gap (37–43). There is one extra paragraph that you do not need to use.

A Race to Remember

Imagine, if you will, charging across sand dunes at a speed of 100 kilometres per hour, with sand flying up at the windscreen while you try to maintain control of the wheel and your navigator attempts to maintain their compass steady at 25 degrees north-northwest, so you don't divert from your course. Now, imagine that scenario taking place over eight hours in a single day and over a period of around 12 days. That is the reality of the world-renowned Dakar Rally.

37	

This year the race took place in Saudi Arabia with a total of 310 vehicles, made up of motorbikes and cars, amongst many other categories, and only 206 of those vehicles crossed the finish line. One individual that made it through this brutal event was Frederique Le Salles for whom it was his second rally. "Although, my first Dakar Rally was five years ago, I've dreamed about coming back ever since. It took me all that time to raise the funds to enter again, and I'm overjoyed to finally return."

38	

As these examples show, the Rally truly does get under people's skin, with the same competitors returning multiple times. This gives them the benefit of experience, which is an essential attribute in this competition. Without the modern necessities of GPS, knowing what the race takes in terms of the trials and tribulations, gives old-timers an important mental advantage in the race, and many taking part more than once because of this.

39	

The event originated from the experience of a man called Thierry Sabine who became so adrift from the course in the 1977 Abidjan-Nice Rally that he realised his detour would make for a great race in itself. The first Dakar Rally started in Dakar in Africa and finished in Paris, skirting around the edges of the Sahara Desert, a gruelling 10,000-kilometre trip.

40	

It is here that I spoke to competitors about their expectations of and concerns for the race, as well as finding out a bit about their preparation for such an unyielding few weeks of fierce motor racing. The responses I received didn't vary wildly – participants' preparation was always meticulous.

41	

One rally driver, who is on his fifth race, told me that he believes a lot of the rally is down to luck. "It takes just a split second to make a mistake, and so, it doesn't matter if you've driven brilliantly for thousands of kilometres, because all you need is one metre to go wrong, and you crash out. It's happened to me twice and it's a completely soul-crushing experience."

42	

Whether this is truly enough to be ready, only time will tell. While the financial rewards for winning aren't publicised (although rumour has it that they are relatively low), the accolade of winning is certainly something money can't buy. However, this doesn't mean that the rally is unprofitable for all, and there are some enterprising routes to make the rally a little more lucrative.

43	

A Such is the commitment to compete that one racer, Chris Cork, sold his house in the UK in order to secure a place on the 2015 Dakar Rally. Unfortunately, he crashed out on the fourth day and had to undergo a difficult recovery procedure for his injuries. Undeterred, he came back the next year to compete, with financial help from well-wishers who were touched by his story.

B Although some entrants go it alone, with the bare-minimum requirements needed to participate, there are many other participants who sign up with companies and receive sponsor bonuses depending on their performance in each round. While finishing a round may be in the hands of fate, it is far more beneficial to do it with sponsorship, as many successful rally winners know.

C As a motorsport reporter, I've been fortunate enough to follow this competition for the last five years, and it never ceases to amaze me how tough and committed each racer is. Rather than a test of driving, or navigation, it is simply an epic feat of endurance. Racers are required to fix their vehicles themselves while on a stage, and there is not even a great probability that they will be able to finish, with most competitors crashing out or breaking down on the route.

D Perhaps the main appeal for these riders is that it offers a sense of adventure that is hard to parallel. The Rally covers lots of harsh terrain and the course is simply a series of written directions. In addition to that, if they don't have any overnight repairs to keep them busy, many drivers find themselves sleeping in tents alongside their vehicles, giving them just enough time to recuperate and get back on the ride. Indeed, unlike many racing events, there is little luxury to be had, and this has always been the case with the Dakar Rally.

E There was lot of focus, as with every rally before, on the terrain, and the best ways to cope with it. 75% of the rally would take place on sand, and a great deal on sand dunes. This means hill climbs and sheer drops, and little ability to spot landmarks to help you know where you are. And remember, if you get your directions wrong, it can take you hours to catch up.

F Fortunately, for many people, the Dakar Rally is a labour of love, but budget can make a significant difference to your opportunities of succeeding. While amateurs may be sleeping aside their vehicles relying on themselves for any repairs, professionals will have a team that can take care of their every need at the end of each stage.

G Although for many years Africa was its home, the location of the Rally has not remained static. It transferred to a different continent altogether, South America, from 2009 to 2019, and more lately to Saudi Arabia, where the vehicles have had to compete with the Middle Eastern deserts, and their scorching days and nearly freezing nights.

H Others are more concerned with how they'll keep their momentum up. "This will be our third race, and we think we've finally discovered what we need to really compete with the best. We've come to realise that the race is about resilience and technical ability, and we've been training with sleep deprivation and motor repair exercises to make sure we've got both these qualities."

You are going to read an article about the bowerbird. For questions 44–53, select the section (A–E) using the separate answer sheet. The section may be selected more than once.

In which section are the following mentioned?

The types of structural layout that bowerbirds use for their homes.	**44**	
How optical illusions play a part in helping the bowerbird attract a mate.	**45**	
The way in which female bowerbirds are impatient when it comes to mate selection.	**46**	
The way in which bowerbirds can be underhanded in obtaining their materials.	**47**	
A physically aggressive mating technique used by the bowerbird.	**48**	
The trial and error involved in making a bower visually attractive.	**49**	
The procedure undertaken by females in mate selection.	**50**	
The fundamental quality that makes a bower a success.	**51**	
How the male bowerbird is almost unequalled in its mating efforts.	**52**	
The transactional nature of the mating behaviour of the male bowerbird.	**53**	

The Unusual Behaviour of the Bowerbird

A

Attracting a mate is one of the fundamental undertakings of life in the animal kingdom, and many creatures go to extreme lengths or exhibit unusual techniques for this very purpose. Take, for example, the common mouse that attracts females by its unique high-pitched songs, or the female flamingo that adds colour to its feathers in order to appeal to the male of the species. Indeed, there is certainly no shortage of weird and wonderful courting rituals in the animal world, but very few of these are more unusual and impressive than those of some species of the bowerbird, who can master DaVinci-like feats of design and knowledge in order to win over its female equivalent. Commonly found in Papua New Guinea and Australia, there are around ninety different species of this bird, and their range is impressive in both size and colour. As such they exhibit a range of efforts and behaviours in order to succeed in finding a mate.

B

Naturally, many types of bowerbird behave in ways common to other species of birds by using physical signs and movements in order to attract others. One such example of this is how, when a female arrives, the male's pupils enlarge and he emits a distinctive call from his throat as a way of indicating his interest in the female. The male, if lucky enough that the female hasn't already departed unimpressed by his intentions, then begins a series of unusual jerking movements with its wings to keep her attention, a display that has been likened to kinds of traditional human dancing such as the Paso Doble. This display can, with some bowerbirds, culminate in perhaps one of the stranger mating techniques in which the male sometimes begins to headbutt the female's chest, certainly not the kind of behaviour you'd expect from an everyday courtship! This is not just an intricate show, but also a well-rehearsed one in which the male frequently changes and adjusts their signs and movements depending on his success rate in attracting a female.

C

As if this wasn't enough, some types of bowerbirds really go the extra mile to find their other halves, engaging in elaborate construction work that takes a considerable amount of forward planning and hard work. Many male bowerbirds erect intricately decorated nests, known as bowers, in a variety of elaborate ways, even stealing from other males' bowers in order to have the most impressive home and be chosen as a mate. These often extremely complex bowers can be built in a tent shape, with the males placing sticks around a small tree, or what could best be described as an igloo shape, with a passageway entrance into a central space full of ornaments. Whatever the type of bower, they all comprise a form of visual enhancement little seen in the animal world and more akin to our own forms of home decoration, albeit in a simpler form.

D

Think, if you will, of a market stall trader who has all his wares on display in an enticing fashion, showing off individual items to potential buyers in the hope of a purchase. The bowerbird's behaviour is reminiscent of this, with their bowers including hundreds of tiny, often colourful objects both natural and manmade, such as flowers, berries, coins and glass. Each of these small pieces is exactingly arranged so as to appeal to females. While the bower's inside is intricately decorated, the male also shows larger objects to the female to catch their attention. And this might occur more than once, as the females go back and forth watching the males' displays and visiting different bowers until they choose the bower that has caught their eye sufficiently to select the male owner as their mate. Females commonly stop at a variety of bowers in order to select their preferred candidate, and some males may be chosen by multiple mates, while others are passed by altogether.

E

Recent investigations into bowerbirds and their bowers have identified that the birds create a pattern of decoration so detailed and clever that they make their bowers appear much bigger than what they actually are when viewed by the female. In fact, the male bowerbird tends to go back and forth into their bowers so they can ensure they've achieved the desired effect, and which they are meticulous about. Recent research shows that if a male's bower is altered in any way, they will painstakingly restore it to their original design. In addition to this, incredibly, their chances of mating are found to be directly related to the regularity of the patterns they create within the bowers. The complexity of this mating behaviour, from both the male and female perspectives, indicates that the bowerbird is a behaviourally complex family of birds, possibly more so than any other bird alive today, and almost certainly the next best home architects after humans.

Name ____________________ **Date** ____________

Part 5

Mark the appropriate answer.

0	A	B	C (marked)	D
31	A	B	C	D
32	A	B	C	D
33	A	B	C	D
34	A	B	C	D
35	A	B	C	D
36	A	B	C	D

Part 6

Add the appropriate answer.

37		38		39		40		41		42		43	

Part 7

Add the appropriate answer.

44		45	
46		47	
48		49	
50		51	
52		53	

Answer key

Test 1 Part 5		Key words from the questions	Clues from the text
31	B	purpose / media, manipulating / examples, intolerance, society / caused, social media / encourage, manners, public	insults traded on social media platforms / sensationalist ways in which the media presents differing public opinions as polarising / The modern world can often feel rude, and people often behave as though they are totally unwilling to consider, or even listen to, views that are not aligned with their own
32	D	opinion / influence, excessive / less important / not easy, justify / always, extremely valuable	mediate between grumpy leaders hell-bent on inflicting their own ideas on the world, diplomacy was once thought of as an art / convey information and messages and negotiate in less inflammatory ways than their leaders might have done / remained on an even keel and avoided conflict at all costs.
33	A	imply / beneficial communication / out-of-date interaction / not worthwhile, modern / effective, political negotiation	whether in our personal lives, in the workplace / bringing back the art of diplomacy could be invaluable. / requires people to put aside their personal desires and work towards a common good.
34	D	developing diplomatic skills / easier, emotional/ everyone, aspire to / too time-consuming / well worth, time and effort	yet with some hard work and determination it is actually straightforward to learn. For people who make a special effort, the benefits will very soon become apparent.
35	C	how, successful, view / optimistic, human condition / overcome suffering / practical perspective / search, happiness. pointless	Diplomats are in essence realists who know full well that relationships, families, jobs and nations will face countless problems. They have accepted this with an air of optimistic resignation and believe that compromise is the only antidote to an imperfect world
36	C	main point / would, more equal, tolerance / best, resolving, fractured / could, positive impact / should, wary, all contexts	They are the undeniable evidence that diplomacy has a lot to offer in illuminating a path to better communication for all of us. Option D is not overtly mentioned, for B the text does not say 'the best approach', and A is incorrect as the text does not say that this would happen.

Test 1 Part 6		Key words from the questions	Clues from the text
37	E	Mindful of this, the long chats I had with my grandparents	if we don't make efforts to unearth experiences of the past from others, they will end up being lost in the mists of time.
38	H	and that fateful evening.	"...That night I watched the great building whose shadow I'd lived under all my life disappear before my very eyes. By morning, there was nothing."
39	A	The only remnants of this one-time marvel	Today, there are few signs
40	D	a far cry from this / All of that was long gone / were getting a bit run down	different types of museum exhibits from around the globe as well as a music hall, a park and a theatre.
41	G	Fortunately, the Earl of Plymouth acquired the palace	plans to auction it off to whoever would pay the most
42	C	this is due to a lack of general awareness	this great treasure is frequently overlooked
43	F	Our parents and grandparents should be encouraged to tell their histories	social first-hand histories are so important / to paint a more vivid picture

Test 1 Part 7		Clues from the questions	Clues from the text
44	E	significant impact / greater need / financial investment	he cites as a concern the funding allocated to / the rich, rather than / developing nations / These glamorous new science awards are a prime example of how scientists in developing nations might be able to benefit from the prize money far more than their western counterparts might.
45	C	Funding / communicators / more worthwhile	Funding that aims to bring science to the public should probably be diverted to the people who have proven track records in engaging people in science.
46	B	new, awards / backed by / a different elite	the world view and associated power of the funders, be they individuals like Zuckerberg or large global corporations. The problem is that these elite minorities are predominately Western with a specific shared world view of the value of knowledge, as well as the aspects of science that are deserving of investment
47	E	unhappy / unequal / investment	warn of the widening gap between the rich and poor among the scientific community / he cites as a concern the funding allocated / of the rich, rather than / developing nations/ Many scientists strongly believe that the West must not just be allowed to dominate and marginalise other nations
48	A	suspicious / principles	this is something that scientists generally tend not to view in a particularly positive light / He is not the only award cynic and others have joined him in voicing concerns
49	A	funded / private	no longer the preserve of prestigious institutions / are paid for by celebrity CEOs such as Mark Zuckerberg and other tech millionaires, with multimillion-dollar prizes
50	D	system / discoveries / not kept pace / changing	In recent times a key criticism of the original Nobel prizes has been the fact that they do not fully represent the way in which science is carried out in modern times / Since the Nobel prizes can only be awarded to three people each year, many hard-working scientists go unnoticed, receiving little or no recognition for their contributions to research and discoveries that simply could not have happened without them.
51	B	impact / generous / financial incentives/ direction / future	younger researchers trying to cut their teeth in a world where funding is increasingly competitive could easily adapt their research to the visions held by the funders of these new awards, visions which may or may not have the interests of humanity as a whole at their heart.
52	D	rooted in cooperation / rather than individuality	most scientific inventions and discoveries are collaborative / dozens of scientists working in cross-cultural teams / rather than individuals working in isolation / the Breakthrough Prize and others have been designed to reward entire teams / wider in their scope and inclusivity.
53	C	prize-winning / needing … funding / low	These huge prizes tend to go to scientists who are already extremely well-funded, and it could easily be argued that they are the least in need of such exorbitant sums.

Test 2 Part 5		Key words from the questions	Clues from the text
31	B	suggest / human relationship / objective truth / know, inaccurate / common meaning, experience / bonding, around us / hard to tell, objectively real	It helps us to realise that we are not alone and have a shared experience / it aids us in organising the abundance of information we receive as human beings.
32	C	past views / common realities / inaccurate / slowly evolved / longevity / illogical	Before the Industrial Revolution, almost all western societies saw reality as quite a different set of concepts. / And as these civilisations, in some form or other, continued in this way for several centuries, we should be sceptical that we, with our modern perception of life,
33	D	feel / information on the internet / establish, accuracy of information / what we choose / less trusting, read / live with, varied quality	there are 'known facts' and 'unknown facts' is something with which we all should probably reconcile ourselves in the modern world. Take the internet, for instance.
34	D	uses / placebo effect / to show / limits, senses / benefits, thinking positively / drawbacks, medical trials / power of pure belief	Placebos – in other words medicines that appear to be a real, but in reality aren't – are often used in clinical trials as a way to measure drug effects, yet sometimes patients' symptoms appear to improve when taking placebos and not the real drugs.
35	A	Donald Hoffman / the way / we / interpret reality / serves, purpose / aids communication / brain deficiency / impedes, understanding	He uses the example of a train / we have given a label in order to attach shared, and indispensable, meanings to the object.
36	B	summarise / their attitude / what we think is real / try to understand / all-knowing, deem ourselves to be / a lot to learn, objective reality / give ourselves up, life's ambiguities	Therefore, to be as bold as to say 'our way is best' is perhaps a little conceited. We know as much as our brains allow and our physical context tells us.

Test 2 Part 6		Key words from the questions	Clues from the text
37	F	However, this hasn't always been the case / Despite / seemed inconceivable … beginning to look like a reality.	meticulous about 'doing things right', which is one of the reasons why this popular toy has stood the test of time.
38	C	In order to do this / rebuilding the organisation / sold all the extras / return to its roots.	What led to this unfortunate state / bad decisions / back to basics and rethink their product strategy.
39	D	By returning to the original ethos / results were clear / turnaround was seen as amazing	This renewed focus / focusing on strengths / not stray from this focus.
40	H	worked with quite a diverse set of companies / paved the way for further innovative Lego Group partnerships	One of the most successful
41	A	engages with children and parents / kinds of toys children like and dislike / marketing to girls	encourage children to develop an interest
42	G	The company became extremely successful / attention to detail	a set of figures aimed at girls was developed
43	B	maintaining customer interest / These extensions	Focusing on what customers like and want / to build customer engagement.

Test 2 Part 7		Clues from the key	Clues from the text
44	C	luck / initially changed / worse	I truly felt I'd won the lottery when they announced that we could take off, but little did I know we'd be stuck on the tarmac at our refuelling point in Bangkok...
45	D	had / stereotypical opinions	I used to treat people who people who took two weeks to go and lay on a beach with contempt, considering them to be unadventurous and uncultured...,
46	E	got to / experience / different / life	everyone has a double and it turns out mine is a Greek soap opera star! Once I realised this, I revelled in the attention, causing a stir wherever I went... After all, who doesn't want to feel special once in a while?
47	B	learned / not / jump to conclusions	I became aware of a suspicious-looking woman / hidden glances at me and whispering to someone on her mobile / she grabbed my wrist and started dragging me towards a strange man! / However, contrary to my suspicions... / Perhaps I should be more trusting in the future
48	C	travel problems / past	I've been at the mercy of a whole host of airline hassles when travelling...
49	B	caused a fuss / something	before I knew it I'd burst into tears, making quite a scene that all the passengers witnessed!
50	E	felt / odd one out	I got the sense that people were giving me furtive glances, / hushed whispers that I suspected were made in my direction / I had a hunch that something wasn't right, and that I was at the centre of it.
51	A	reliant / one person	a guide was at our disposal to deal with any eventualities... / at least keep us alive! ..., we'd have been toast if it hadn't been for him.
52	A	in awe / surroundings	My overwhelming recollection, though, is what a feast for my senses the jungle was – at night it is like an orchestra of the natural world.
53	D	thought / ready for anything	Of course, as a seasoned adventurer, I was prepared for such eventualities and so grabbed my mobile to call for help, only to see I had no reception.

Test 3 Part 5		Key words from the questions	Clues from the text
31	A	bus journeys / adverse, ... her own decision-making / overnight ... draining / annoyed ... neglected /scheduled ... surprisingly well	Even then I knew that choosing the most inexpensive bus company was risky, but their bus was scheduled to depart immediately and I'd been impatient yet again. I was furious with myself. Of course, by then it was too late
32	D	suggests / veteran / no incidents / luxury ... closer to home / broaden horizons	not everything could go smoothly. That was the reason / I was supposed to be growing as a person / allow me to discover things about myself that had lain hidden in my overly stressful London lifestyle.
33	C	Before / convinced ... healing / hoped ... expectations / sceptical ... life-changing / believed ... key ... troubles	Initially, I'd been suspicious of this / Why I imagined that disconnecting / wouldn't be positive I have no idea / I'd told anyone willing to listen that I disputed the fact that travel could be transformational.
34	B	change / record accurately / reflective ...thoughtful / less compelled ...write / better ... understanding ... cultures	my entries began to take on a different vibe / more descriptive pieces with observations and a gradual emergence of emotive responses to the world around me.
35	A	implies ... accepted / benefit ... mental health / linguistic ... matched / sorry ... Sofia's plight / experience ... identical	noticed the server as she happily bustled around, greeting all the customers, chatting and laughing as she went, and it occurred to me that I couldn't recall the last time I'd had fun at work. / And at that moment, right there in the café, I realised that the proposition was too tempting to resist.
36	C	overall effect / more outgoing / enhanced ...life skills / reconsider ...goals / regrets ... life	As I somewhat nervously stepped into the sunshine to greet my first customers, I tried to picture my office and flat back in London and noticed that the images seemed to be fading just a little around the edges.

Test 3 Part 6		Key words from the questions	Clues from the text
37	G	Fashion designers have much more freedom with digital garments and can play around in more creative ways	customers can be far more imaginative; in fact, the sky is the limit when it comes to designs in the digital arena
38	F	The most obvious of these is its sustainability.	What is new, though, is the growing number of advantages of digital over physical fashion.
39	D	Costs can be decreased further through / more collections that will start to address individual lifestyle needs	costs that are associated with making samples, having face-to-face meetings and other logistical concerns can be drastically reduced
40	A	While some of the new trends have started to emerge, such as the rise in demand for leisurewear	This is likely to become more important in the near future as companies rush to meet consumers' needs / create new types of clothing that allow for more comfort and ease of movement
41	H	By putting the individual at the heart of digital fashion	They could also start asking for a garment to be copied using different material / The possibilities for creativity are endless and customers could end up with the clothes that they have always dreamed of owning yet could never find.
42	E	Currently, this work is done by people and it is still quite a time-consuming process	the technology is not quite as advanced as people might think.
43	C	imaginary online characters / growing desire to do the same with online selves too.	As a result, digital clothing remains quite expensive / video game sector can shed some light on customer engagement with digital fashion

Test 3 Part 7		Clues from the key	Clues from the text
44	**C**	connection / muscles / combat / cold climates	The discovery of this protein has also contributed to ongoing research over the last decade into the ability of humans to tolerate cold climates.
45	**D**	change / environment / trigger / alteration	As homo sapiens began to move north from Africa over 40,000 years ago they would have started to settle in colder climates, and this would have caused a change in their metabolisms in order to manage living in these new conditions.
46	**A**	Studies / athletes / answer / question	For a long time, scientists have wondered why some people are better than others at tolerating the cold, and recent research into why athletes from different parts of the globe excel in different sports may have shed some light on the issue.
47	**F**	New medicines / combining / fields	...like many scientific enquiries, provided innovation in medicine by incorporating studies into a much newer field, that of sports science.
48	**B**	proportion / types / same / irrespective / training	Humans have different combinations of these two muscle types that are set at birth and cannot be changed through exercise...
49	**E**	lacking / protein / less able / healthy	If people without the specific protein are able to maintain their body temperatures more easily, this suggest that, unless they follow a healthy diet and exercise regularly, the risk of obesity and associated problems such as diabetes may be considerably higher for them.
50	**D**	Slow-twitch / better / regulating / temperature	...slow-twitch muscles, which are more efficient and allow people to tolerate colder temperatures for longer periods of time.
51	**B**	excellence / due / biological / individual	...people who end up becoming athletes, where the ratio of fast-twitch and slow-twitch muscles is disproportionate compared to the rest of the population, where it is about 50:50. In essence, then, these people are born to be athletes.
52	**F**	higher proportion / slow-twitch / mobility problems	...those with the gene mutation and therefore without the protein) may injure themselves more frequently and easily as they get older. Given that fast-twitch muscles handle explosive movements such as falling, it follows that older people who do not have as many fast-twitch muscles may be more susceptible to accidents.
53	**E**	Treatment / precise / result / muscle research	...scientists may be able to develop medication that is more effective for different groups of patients.

Test 4 Part 5		Key words from the questions	Clues from the text
31	B	writer's reaction / horror / avoid watching / love-hate relationship / fear experienced / terrifying ordeal	If, like me, / hidden behind your cushion anticipating the climax to some petrifying scene / can't help but watch horror films without the faintest idea of why they're putting themselves through such an ordeal.
32	D	horror films / sense of insecurity/anticipation/misadventure/accomplishment	we can also get a feeling of pride once we've endured the entire film, as if we've confronted the horror ourselves!
33	A	'ridiculous' / imagine ourselves as the characters / how we react, plots in horror films / some characters react to situations / compare, to, real-life scenarios	As ridiculous as it sounds / we naturally set about contemplating how we would react if we were in the shoes of those in danger on screen
34	C	writer's perspective / horror film victims / see the danger / limited abilities / predicably dim / stereotypical	These formulaic moves enable us to conclude / more wary than the short-sighted sap we see on the screen
35	B	horror films scare people who / more realistic / receptive, story / negative beliefs / see themselves, emotional	Some people also have a better ability to suspend belief than others / those who tend to get wrapped up in the plot (and take a leap of faith that these things could really happen) can find such films unbearable.
36	D	advice / at the end / think, why / realise, how, improbably / laugh, at, ridiculous / watch, practical angle	baddie / standing behind that curtain for who knows how many hours / got caught in the curtain / had cramp / Sometimes, asking the most pragmatic questions makes a horror film turn into a joke.

Test 4 Part 6		Key words from the questions	Clues from the text
37	B	I actually started writing fairly late in life / I hadn't the slightest desire to be famous.	I'm particularly satisfied with how this, my fourth non-fiction work on art has turned out / it demonstrates my overall development as a writer.
38	A	This developed into a stronger desire for recognition / my entrance to the literary world would come through an altogether more unconventional route.	Given all that, it seems strange that I find myself here / and a vague idea of perhaps being published one day
39	H	I have always had a passion for art / although I don't have an artistic bone in my body, unlike my sister, Louisa,	When I compare it to those of my contemporaries, my experience seems extraordinary nowadays.
40	F	It was a real success and I was delighted to have taken part / set the wheels in motion to entirely change my life / Rebecca Martin who worked for the online arts magazine, *Palette*.	One evening I got a call from her / upcoming exhibition brochure / could I give her a hand, or at least some guidance
41	D	Well, to be honest I didn't know what to think / filled me with terror / messaged my sister	she managed to track me down, first through contacting the gallery and then my sister
42	G	Over the following months I devoted every spare moment of my time to attending exhibitions	Louisa persuaded me to take the plunge, and to my surprise, that is exactly what I did
43	C	As my readership grew, so did my reputation as a writer	After that first summer, I was hooked on writing

Test 4 Part 7		Clues from the key	Clues from the text
44	**B**	Switching / plant / easier / cultivate	From their perspective, they are better off growing oil palms because palm oil is less labour intensive to produce than rubber.
45	**C**	Producers / responsible / production	many large rubber buyers, including the world's largest tire companies, have signed up to an organisation campaigning for sustainable rubber / aims to send a clear message to governments that clarifies what corporations are not prepared to accept.
46	**A**	unaware / importance / rubber / manufacturing	Make this question about a naturally occurring material and the responses are more varied, ranging from wood to iron to coal. Yet the raw material that we rely on most / is of course rubber.
47	**B**	livelihoods / producers / insecure	This means that small farmers are at the mercy of these price fluctuations, and many of them cannot continue when prices are kept low for long periods of time.
48	**D**	reducing dependence / overseas	a country that currently relies heavily on the Asian rubber supply and which is actively looking for ways to reduce this reliance given the issues mentioned above.
49	**B**	mass planting / controversial	Governments in some countries have cleared vast areas of forest to grow rubber trees for profit alone, and there is a strong view that this kind of behaviour should not be encouraged.
50	**C**	fear / rubber trees / destroyed	Some scientists believe that with the amount of goods and people constantly traversing the world, it is only a matter of time before this disease arrives in Asia too / the world's supply of rubber could vanish almost overnight and there is little that can be done to prevent such a disaster.
51	**A**	production / different / other materials	Although the extraction of many other raw materials such as stone or timber is done via large corporations on an industrial scale, this is not the case with rubber. In fact, quite the opposite is true
52	**D**	biological methods / increase / cultivation / options	Researchers are working on breeding strains of the plant that could be grown on a much larger scale so as to avoid the current world reliance on a plant whose future is far from secure.
53	**D**	cost-effective / replacements	a couple of plants that could potentially be used as substitutes. The most financially viable of these is guayule

Test 5 Part 5		Key words from the questions	Clues from the text
31	C	objectives, changed recently / prefer teams without, hierarchies / sights higher than previous generations / fewer, motivated by responsibility / management, more attractive	Not anymore, though / A survey in 2019 reported that considerably less than half of the thousand employees interviewed / saw management as a desirable career path.
32	A	challenge, early managers / discipline / respect / control / training	Conversely, the new, less skilled workers had little demanded of them, except to follow orders precisely, and this gave rise to the role of manager since the character of this workforce was often ill equipped for the nature of factory work, which resulted in frequent absences and accidents.
33	D	ironic / positive attitude, technology / desire, old techniques / technology, replace managers / changes, full circle	this may be causing a return to the old ways of working. / It could even be argued that technology is better / at these tasks than human beings. But there is another point / nature of many modern jobs is more akin to the role of the old craftsmen and women.
34	C	traditional, disappearing / expertise, out of date / knowledge, disputed / no … purpose / not … team players	self-organise in small teams without the need for a manager / and managers are increasingly viewed with irritation as they try to impose their own ideas on a project without having the necessary expert understanding. Many companies nowadays have self-managing teams / shifted the manager's role to that of mentor.
35	C	future / positive / career to be avoided / Yet to be defined / not … stand test of time	managers will have to develop new skills that they could possibly use in / Some of these skills could include
36	B	concludes / provide, wider, benefits / relationship, individuals, evolved / satisfaction … through … belonging / value interpersonal skills	this clearly highlights the difference between the old and new practices. Previously / controlling of others / while nowadays people are more inward looking with a focus on personal fulfilment

Test 5 Part 6		Key words from the questions	Clues from the text
37	G	Sir Douglas Mawson and his team didn't have such luxuries	I dressed in layers of thermal and waterproof clothing
38	D	It's essentially a wonderful social history / nature is constantly trying the reclaim this settlement	small details as their names on their bunks, and names of familiar places they could think about while there. / continual efforts have been made to preserve the structure
39	F	However, and although this is one of a smattering of structures of historic significance / it is far from unusual as abandoned buildings in Antarctica go / 5,000 structures	six surviving sites from what is known as the Heroic Era of Antarctic Explorations / This may seem incredible, seeing as Antarctica has no permanent human population.
40	A	The land and the wildlife that live on it are extremely sensitive / coupled with the careless introduction of human activity, can leave indelible effects / irresponsible disposal of waste for human-related activities.	The fact that this beautiful wilderness is littered with disused buildings is something that is extremely problematic and the focus of international action. / things are changing / more general awareness / the Madrid Protocol
41	C	One reason for this is that these obligations do not apply to buildings / another policy decision that perhaps caused the initial boom	Madrid Protocol / rules on commercial activity /still thousands of empty outposts to see there. / 1959 Antarctic Treaty / only countries conducting substantial research activity in Antarctica could have a vote

42	H	Nowadays, the continent is peppered with run-down structures / We can only imagine what Sir Douglas Mawson would have thought	saw heightened interest in the area / The footprint of the Mawson expedition would have been relatively minor
43	B	There is no easy resolution to this dilemma.	these elements are necessary / but they are certainly at odds with preservation of the natural environment.

Test 5 Part 7		**Clues from the key**	**Clues from the text**
44	D	prioritised / local businesses / outset	so we gave priority to performers and caterers who were local residents themselves.
45	A	organisers / indifferent / certain festival-goers	fail to provide adequate access for people in my situation. / it's discrimination as it feels like the organisers are either ignoring us or can't be bothered to find solutions to our access problems.
46	B	explanation / dislike / effects	Getting to some of the small villages where these festivals are located is extremely challenging for buses and caravans, and local residents are none too pleased with the disruption all this causes to their everyday lives.
47	D	staging / commitment	but of course that was when we realised just how much work the organisation would entail. We were slightly daunted by the prospect to be honest
48	C	downside / range of performers	I always end up having to miss something I want to see as a result of performance clashes. / sometimes I feel a little short changed, like I haven't had real value for money because I've had to miss some performances or talks that I was really keen on seeing.
49	A	imbalance / facilities	fail to provide adequate access for people in my situation. This is especially true when compared to other music and performance venues, such as concert halls and theatres where disabled access is a legal requirement nowadays.
50	B	preference / formal approach	these events are far better than sitting in a field with a picnic listening to music because here there are tables and chairs, and proper plates and glasses,
51	D	dissatisfied / narrow target audience	complaining about a lack of provision for families with children, especially those from poorer backgrounds or those with disabilities.
52	B	financial benefits	Food tourism brings visitors from far and wide, and although it's boosted our local economy considerably over the last couple of decades
53	C	fussy / type / comfortable	However, that's not to say that I never attend any. I'm just selective and ensure that I research an event thoroughly beforehand to evaluate its suitability.

Test 6 Part 5		Key words from the questions	Clues from the text
31	C	the writer feel, his work / / as much as he'd hoped / being wasted / wasn't appreciated / below him	most nights I felt like I received about as much recognition as the furniture did.
32	B	why, go back, parents / take a break, city life / help, task / spend time / look after	they couldn't realistically undertake a task like that without some assistance with the bulk of it / I knew my assistance would be invaluable
33	A	how, the writer, feel about his life / hadn't turned out, expected / feels bitter, choices / regrets, optimism / thinks, destined to be	was a far cry from the future I'd dreamed of as a hopeful child for my forty-five-year-old self.
34	C	He, his dad, afternoon / talking about, found, attic / describing, world changed since / looking back, their childhoods, fondness / sorting through	we spent the afternoon browsing through the pages while he reminisced over the good old days. It even triggered my own recollections!
35	D	writer's initial attitude, comics / particularly memorable / give, happiness / shouldn't be thrown out / nothing out of the ordinary	a box of old superhero comics / I packed them into the trunk of my truck / with the other junk / the old clutter
36	B	sums up, main idea / never too late / turn around / finding happiness / fresh start	behind on my rent and my music career appeared to be at an effective standstill / The future, instead of looking like an amazing blank canvas, felt like a bleak and empty space / the tide was about to turn / We couldn't believe our eyes / entire future was transformed by my parent's generosity, a shopkeeper's honesty, and one long-forgotten old comic!

Test 6 Part 6		Key words from the questions	Clues from the text
37	E	this bleak interpretation / in the field of science / where women have usually taken a back seat,	phrase more literally refers to / yet it also infers the disheartening idea that perhaps women
38	H	in one of the winner's memoirs / towards her /	Rosalind Franklin / research was overlooked / The acclaim for the discovery, however, and even the Nobel Prize, went to three men / Incidents like this
39	D	However / the views on female scientists are too deeply embedded in the scientific community for the situation to be rectified overnight. / male / perceived as being of higher scientific quality / men are more desirable as collaboration partners.	One of Rossiter's aims has been that a renewed focus on successes of female scientists in history may encourage more women to enter the field of science. / Still, efforts continue
40	F	For instance, try finding out about 'the Dean Method' online. A quick google	rectifying past injustices by amending search-engine results to reflect real contributions
41	A	The Matthew Effect can be summarised as the way in which disproportionate recognition is attributed	perhaps the defining factor is simply the historically unequal power relationship
42	C	One effort we can all make / encourage a shift in people's attitudes / that doesn't mean things should remain the same in the years to come.	maybe it will be a little harder to find those men who were overlooked in favour of someone with a greater stature / Perhaps science will never reach an ideal / opening this subject up for reflection and discussion is essential

43	**G**	you make up part of the world we share, and a sea change only happens through the individual shifts in people's opinions.	reflection and discussion is essential / and both the terms 'the Matilda Effect' and 'the Matthew Effect' by their very use are making inroads into highlighting inequalities.

Test 6 Part 7		**Clues from the key**	**Clues from the text**
44	**D**	need to focus /reduce one-time consumption.	With this in mind, we should ask ourselves how one excess can be used to give power to something else. This kind of sustainability
45	**B**	A fix / varying / effort	This might consist of making tweaks or, in certain contexts, starting from scratch
46	**B**	reputation / overlooks their positive aspects	Cities are often seen in a bad light, but I think this is undeserved, because they offer so much to so many.
47	**A**	acknowledgement / solution may be disagreeable / some	This might seem less than ideal for the average city dweller
48	**E**	designed in a way that makes us feel detached	cities are like these huge sprawls, just spreading and spreading / the bigger plot each homeowner has and the more spacious / this really has a negative effect / makes us more isolated
49	**D**	How / people / more integrated	creating and promoting more sharing and communal practices, like coworking spaces or apartment buildings with common spaces
50	**C**	Some people / ignoring problems / should be tackling	The powers that be seem disinclined to do anything but sweep this under the carpet
51	**E**	Cities left /grow unchecked	Cities today have one fundamental problem that we need to curb, and that is urban sprawl. / cities are like these huge sprawls, just spreading and spreading
52	**A**	Future enhancements / determined by / construction	We're going to be somewhat reliant on technology to help us with this, by, for example, developing materials that we can use to build higher...
53	**C**	reputation of / the reality of cities / different	We need to face up to the fact that most cities aren't the glorious places that they are painted to be, and that, for the majority of the inhabitants, the streets aren't paved with gold.

Test 7 Part 5		Key words from the questions	Clues from the text
31	B	argues / forecasting, locations, pointless / approached, shortage, wrong angle/ causes, too complex / few, solutions, viable	rather than lamenting the journey to this point / better off focusing on solutions / causes have been written about extensively and are very well understood / not the case for the solutions.
32	C	infrastructure collaborations / Local, valued / Costs excessive / Planning, fundamental, Resources inadequate	Solutions for water scarcity should primarily be context-specific / For example, there is no point / Too often collaborations on projects like this turn into vanity projects for the foreign companies / Workable solutions will need to understand / will likely be a combination
33	A	water meters, not promoted/ politically damaging / costs, beyond, poor / media, interested, other solutions / efficiency, questioned	by installing water meters in homes, something that has not been widely reported in the press / little incentive for governments to encourage uptake / any change would negatively affect voters on low incomes and families.
34	D	people should be taught, scarcity / information, online / impact, meat industry / government, campaigns / access, research	A better alternative / for governments to invest in educating their populations. / Education on water conservation methods should come from a commitment to ensuring people have the relevant scientific evidence presented to them, otherwise they will be unable to make informed decisions.
35	D	simple solutions / more effective, environment / results, quickly / straightforward processes / studies, uptake, higher	small lifestyles changes / ordinary people can do without disrupting their lives / Research from behavioural science has shown that when people have to opt into a system the likelihood of their doing so is reduced because of the increased effort involved.
36	A	point, tackling, scarcity / Controlling, commercial, essential / Human beings, not interfere, natural / Countries, strict laws, progress / Some, measures, ill-advised	certain ecosystems / forests, marshes and wetlands, that naturally process, collect, and filter water / Unfortunately, the practices of many commercial industries are at odds with conservation strategies / Making laws to protect these natural systems / it's high time that governments stepped up and took control

Test 7 Part 6		Key words from the questions	Clues from the text
37	C	It was then that it dawned on me / I longed desperately for my eyes to remain shut	I became dizzily aware / This felt all too realistic / my senses, and my brain started whirring
38	F	This is what prompted my visits with Dr Potter / come around in the lane of a highway	I was in terrible danger / made a run for it / appeared as a nightmare vision / This is one of the most disturbing cases
39	H	Pinpointing where it started was more difficult than I imagined / lay out a history	Tell me everything / scribbled away, interjecting with the odd nod or question to clarify any vagaries
40	A	what lay before me / sensors placed all over my body / video equipment recording my every move	starting with a visit to a sleep clinic / It turned out to be far easier than keeping track of my days
41	E	in quite a bad temper on my return visit / took it out on the doctor a little / such laborious tasks / a stern response in return	took up so much of my day / making my moods, and condition, worse / It seemed I had really angered him
42	B	Then, snapping me out of my fixation on a nearby willow and back to the present situation, he delivered his epiphany. / stress / my workload had gotten on top of me	he leafed through my diary / I fidgeted / contemplating / this was true
43	D	as I've learned to make essential changes to my lifestyle.	essential to put your own wellbeing first.

Test 7 Part 7		Clues from the key	Clues from the text
44	B	suggests / could / upskill / expectations	I am slightly concerned / impact on less technologically minded designers / clients / expect a basic level of proficiency with design apps.
45	C	not convinced / worth speculating / future	no point in trying to predict the outcomes / with any certainty. / end is in sight / oversimplification
46	A	supports / wide customer base	what is changing is exciting / open up the sector to more people. / used to only be accessible by a select few / now more egalitarian
47	D	connection / social mobility	important for more people to have access / because reflects a society that has improved living conditions for its citizens.
48	D	disappointed / bland / everyone	this horrible period / beige stage / desire to express their individuality / identical. The retail landscape is entirely uninspiring
49	A	technology / transform	Apps / are going to revolutionise how we do things / image apps / really opened up the possibilities
50	E	suggests / more environmentally friendly	period of re-evaluation / rejecting certain materials / focusing on innovative ways to be sustainable
51	C	future / comparable / another industry	There are considerable similarities to what went on in the travel sector / Likewise, interior design
52	E	predicts / designers / work / other professionals	more collaboration between interior designers and engineers
53	B	little evidence / technology / replace / designers	The latest market analysis is not telling us that people want / high-tech anytime soon. In fact, quite the opposite seems to be true if you look carefully at the research.

Test 8 Part 5		Key words from the questions	Clues from the text
31	B	business idea, born out of / frustration, lack / desire, purpose / discovery, talent / daydreaming, problem	Daniel had been busy carving out an impressive career in marketing consultancy but had recently become disillusioned by the industry and was looking for something more meaningful.
32	A	became friends/ attention to detail, important / shared attitudes, creativity / questioned, taught / emotionally connected, objects	which was how their paths had first crossed. Selina had joined the engineering club at university and one evening Daniel walked in on the hunt for a specific tool. Noticing the intricate bicycle carvings poking out of his rucksack, she'd asked to examine them, and then proceeded to ask all sorts of questions about their construction, which delighted him no end.
33	C	Daniel, depict, first meeting / not memorable / omits, details / exaggerates, comic / hilarious	Later, Daniel would always say that this gesture was what cemented their friendship forever, although she suspected it was artistic license, a way of adding a touch of humour to an otherwise fairly unremarkable story.
34	C	business, difficult, started / Expanding, range, products / where, advertise / Widening, customer / Identifying, market	At the outset, their only customers were friends, family and colleagues who, whilst impressed by the quality of the toys, were obviously buying them as a show of support and therefore they couldn't quite work out whether a wider market existed.
35	A	Selina, feel, development, business / remarkable / administration, tiresome / worried, stability / surprised, growth	Now they had an actual business with offices and employees, and all the associated tedious tasks that those things brought. At some level Selina struggled to see the business as real and, on some mornings, found herself standing at the entrance looking out at their office and marvelling at its sheer existence
36	D	Selina, feel, end / Delighted, acquiring, business / Concerned, without consulting her / Amused, Daniel, explain, stranger/ Relieved, same wavelength	"Selina, this is Joanne Hardy, she's an investor and is interested in purchasing part of our business." After we had sat down and exchanged some pleasantries, Joanne turned to Selina and said, "So, how did you two meet?" "Well, ...", Daniel began. At this moment Selina felt a wave of relaxation surge over her...

Test 8 Part 6		Key words from the questions	Clues from the text
37	C	As a motorsport reporter, I've been fortunate enough to follow this competition...	That is the reality of the world-renowned Dakar Rally.
38	A	Such is the commitment to compete that one racer, Chris Cork...	Frederique Le Salles / I've dreamed about coming back ever since. It took me all that time to raise the funds to enter again..." / As these examples show, the Rally truly does get under people's skin...
39	D	Perhaps the main appeal for these riders... / ...this has always been the case with the Dakar Rally.	...and many taking part more than once because of this. / The event originated...
40	G	Although for many years Africa was its home, / ...lately to Saudi Arabia...	The first Dakar started in Dakar in Africa and finished in Paris, skirting around the edges of the Sahara Desert... / It is here...
41	E	There was lot of focus, as with every rally before, on the terrain / best ways to cope with it.	The responses I received didn't vary wildly – participants' preparation was always meticulous.

42	H	Others are more concerned with how they'll keep their momentum up. / ...we've been training with sleep deprivation and motor repair exercises...	One rally driver... / ...rally is down to luck. / Whether this is truly enough to be ready...
43	B	...some entrants go it alone / ...other participants who sign up with companies... / ...receive sponsor bonuses...	...some enterprising routes to make the rally a little more lucrative.

Test 8 Part 7		**Clues from the key**	**Clues from the text**
44	C	types / structural layout / bowerbirds	These often extremely complex bowers can be built in a tent shape, / or what could best be described as an igloo shape, with a passageway entrance...
45	E	How optical illusions / helping / attract a mate	create a pattern of decoration so detailed and clever, that they make their bowers appear much bigger than what they actually are when viewed by the female. / tends to go back and forth into their bowers so they can ensure they've achieved the desired effect...
46	B	way / female bowerbirds / impatient / mate selection	The male, if lucky enough that the female hasn't already departed unimpressed by his intentions...
47	C	way / bowerbirds / be underhanded / obtaining / materials	even stealing from other males' bowers, in order to have the most impressive home and be chosen as a mate.
48	B	physically aggressive mating technique	in which the male sometimes begins to headbutt the female's chest...
49	E	trial and error / making a bower visually attractive	In fact, the male bowerbird tends to go back and forth into their bowers so they can ensure they've achieved the desired effect...
50	D	procedure / females / mate selection	And this might occur more than once, as the females go back and forth watching the males' displays and visiting different bowers until they choose the bower that has caught their eye... / commonly stop at a variety of bowers in order to select their preferred candidate...
51	E	fundamental quality / bower / success	...incredibly, their chances of mating are found to be directly related to the regularity of the patterns...
52	A	How / male / almost unequalled / mating efforts	no shortage of weird and wonderful courting rituals in the animal world, but very few of these are more unusual and impressive than those of some species of the bowerbird...
53	D	transactional nature / mating behaviour / male	Think, if you will, of a market stall trader, who has all his wares on display in an enticing fashion, showing off individual items to potential buyers in the hope of a purchase. The bowerbird's behaviour is reminiscent of this, with their bowers including hundreds of tiny, often colourful, objects both natural and manmade, such as flowers, berries, coins and glass. / While the bower's inside is intricately decorated, the male also shows larger objects to the female to catch their attention.

Bonus content

Cambridge C2 Proficiency
Use of English: Parts 1–4

Test 2

For questions 1–8, read the text below and decide which answer best fits each gap. In the separate answer sheet, mark the appropriate answer (A, B, C or D).

The Benefits of Nostalgia

The other day, over coffee, my friend Angela confided her concerns about becoming overly nostalgic for her past. She'd never struck me as a **(1)**_______________ person, so I was naturally concerned. I decided to mention a fascinating video I'd watched online about the subject.

Apparently, doctors used to have the misguided **(2)**_______________ that nostalgia was a mental illness. However, in the last couple of decades psychologists have **(3)**_______________ doubt on this. They've realised that it's actually a **(4)**_______________ effective form of self-treatment in times of anxiety or isolation. In the video, a psychologist described how people derive **(5)**_______________ from reliving pleasant past experiences. This is because the process releases positive chemicals in the brain that help build motivation for the future.

So, equipped with my newfound facts, I launched into the conversation hoping to make Angela feel less miserable. She started nodding enthusiastically, saying this explanation really **(6)**_______________ the nail on the head. Her working environment had become quite stressful, mainly due to some issues with the company's finances, and it was really beginning to take **(7)**_______________ toll on her. This was causing the nostalgic feelings, and the result was that she'd lost **(8)**_______________ of the bigger picture of her life.

Anyway, she promised to watch the video herself and I hope it benefits her, too.

1	**A**	bland	**B**	sentimental	**C**	pathetic	**D**	longing
2	**A**	belief	**B**	conclusion	**C**	deduction	**D**	intuition
3	**A**	cast	**B**	dropped	**C**	thrown	**D**	shed
4	**A**	realistically	**B**	conclusively	**C**	remarkably	**D**	unanimously
5	**A**	relief	**B**	comfort	**C**	caution	**D**	freedom
6	**A**	tapped	**B**	struck	**C**	chopped	**D**	hit
7	**A**	its	**B**	some	**C**	a	**D**	all
8	**A**	standard	**B**	sight	**C**	perspective	**D**	outlook

For questions 9–16, read the text below and decide which word best fits each gap. Use only one word for each gap. In the separate answer sheet, write your answers in capital letters, using one box per letter.

A Female President?

In 2016, the USA missed out on having its first female president. However, **(9)**_______________ most people don't realise is that in the early 20th century one woman single-handedly assumed the presidential role, **(10)**_______________ all but name. Although never officially elected, as the wife of US President Woodrow Wilson, Edith Wilson secretly governed the entire country for over a year while her husband was seriously ill.

Upon **(11)**_______________, it was love at first sight between Edith and Woodrow, and she soon became one of his trusted advisors, despite having no political experience, a development with which Wilson's administrative team were ill at **(12)**_______________ to say the least. Despite objections, Edith and Woodrow soon married and she became engaged **(13)**_______________ helping the President with his work, unofficially, with full access to all kinds of classified materials.

When Woodrow had a stroke, Edith would not contemplate that he should resign from the role as President and have the Vice President step in. She decided instead to cover **(14)**_______________ his illness by taking on his duties in secret. According to her and her personal physicians, Woodrow was working from his bedroom, and she insisted that all presidential work come **(15)**_______________ her, even firing staff members who disobeyed. Many at the time claimed it was clear to see the lack of governance, but all things considered, for a working-class girl who had to **(16)**_______________ it by ear, she didn't do a bad job.

For questions 17–24, use the stem word on the right to form the correct word that fills each gap. In the separate answer sheet, write your answers in capital letters, using one box per letter.

Job Interview Advice

Nerves affect even the most confident person before a job interview, which is why preparation and attitude are vital. Being chosen for an interview means that, on paper, you have all the necessary **(17)**______________. So, when	**QUALIFY**
preparing remember that you are **(18)**______________ of the interviewer's time. However, so are the rest of the interviewees, which means you need stand out.	**WORTH**
While you have fulfilled the essential criteria on the job specification, look at the list of **(19)**______________ attributes closely. Focusing on these will	**DESIRE**
(20)______________ your thinking in preparation for the interview.	**SHARP**
Background research on the organisation prior to your interview will be helpful, too, as it will enable you to better **(21)**______________ to the interviewer. This helps to understand the type of person they want to fit the organisational culture. Another characteristic to highlight is	**RELATIONSHIP**
that of being **(22)**______________ as it is a highly valued trait nowadays. Just remember that you'll need concrete examples.	**RESOURCE**
Lastly, is your approach on the day. From your initial step inside the building present a picture of **(23)**______________ to everyone you encounter, from the reception staff to senior management. Even though you may be nervous, whatever happens in the interview will be a learning curve. Try to convince yourself that this	**CHEER**
could be a **(24)**______________ experience. You never know, you might just get the job!	**PLEASURE**

For questions 25–30, complete the second sentence, using the word given, so that it has a similar meaning to the first sentence. Do not change the word provided and use between three and eight words in total. In the separate answer sheet, write your answers in capital letters, using one box per letter.

25 The director was surprised, as there wasn't any indication that he'd be the winner.

WHATSOEVER

There was ______________________ the director would win the award.

26 Joyce had a difficult life as a child and so joined the army at a young age.

CONTEND

Joyce joined the army so young, because she had a ______________________ growing up.

27 I love oysters, but I know they are not to everyone's taste.

NOSES

A lot of people ______________________, but I think they're delicious.

28 The bakery continues to be successful despite the new supermarket in town.

STRONG

Even though there is a new supermarket in town, the bakery ______________________.

29 Peter had spent so much time practising that there was no doubt he'd pass his driving test.

BOUND

By the amount of practice he's done, Peter ______________________ his driving test.

30 We haven't confirmed the reports yet, so would you mind waiting before you make any announcements?

HOLD

Could ______________________ announcements until we can confirm the reports?

Answer sheet: Cambridge C2 Proficiency
Use of English

Test No. ☐

Mark out of 36 ☐

Name ______________________ **Date** ______________

Part 1: Multiple choice

8 marks

Mark the appropriate answer (A, B, C or D).

0	A	**B**	C	D

1	A	B	C	D
2	A	B	C	D
3	A	B	C	D
4	A	B	C	D
5	A	B	C	D
6	A	B	C	D
7	A	B	C	D
8	A	B	C	D

Part 2: Open cloze

8 marks

Write your answers in capital letters, using one box per letter.

0	B	E	C	A	U	S	E				

9											
10											
11											
12											
13											
14											
15											
16											

Part 3: Word formation

8 marks

Write your answers in capital letters, using one box per letter.

17

18

19

20

21

22

23

24

Part 4: Key word transformation

12 marks

Write your answers in capital letters, using one box per letter.

25

26

27

28

29

30

Printed in Great Britain
by Amazon